D1595884

EDWIN BOOTH'S PERFORMANCES

The

Mary Isabella Stone Commentaries

Theatre and Dramatic Studies, No. 59

Oscar G. Brockett, Series Editor

Professor of Drama and Holder of the
Z. T. Scott Family Chair in Drama
The University of Texas at Austin

Other Titles in This Series

EDWIN BOOTH'S PERFORMANCES

— The —
Mary Isabella Stone Commentaries

Edited & annotated by
Daniel J. Watermeier

With a foreword by
Charles H. Shattuck

U·M·I Research Press

Ann Arbor / London

Produced and distributed by
UMI Research Press
an imprint of
University Microfilms Inc.
Ann Arbor, Michigan 48106

Library of Congress Cataloging in Publication Data

Stone, Mary Isabella.
  Edwin Booth's performances : the Mary Isabella Stone commentaries / edited and annotated by Daniel J. Watermeier.
    p. cm.—(Theatre and dramatic studies ; no. 59)
  Includes bibliographical references.
  ISBN 0-8357-1974-X (alk. paper)
    1. Shakespeare, William, 1564-1616—Stage history—1800-1950.
  2. Booth, Edwin, 1833-1893—Criticism and interpretation.
  3. Shakespeare, William, 1564-1616—Characters—Hamlet.
  4. Shakespeare, William, 1564-1616—Characters—Iago.
  I. Watermeier, Daniel J. II. Series: Theatre and dramatic studies ;
  no. 59.
  PR3112.S76   1989
  792.9'5—dc20   89-37325

British Library CIP data is available.

Contents

Appendix

Foreword

In 1969 I published a book entitled *The Hamlet of Edwin Booth*. What prompted that effort was the emergence from the files of the Folger Shakespeare Library of a manuscript, some 60,000 words long, which meticulously recorded and annotated Booth's every word, gesture, movement, and facial expression in his 1870 performances of Hamlet

The faithful compiler of of this record was a young man named Charles W. Clarke (1848–1940), a native of Connecticut, who had come into New York City in 1865 or 1866, hoping, it appears, to pursue a career in letters. Already at seventeen he had sold a short story. This might be the open sesame to some congenial employment in...

But we need not speculate. He could not live on rejection slips alone. At eighteen he took a job with the commercial firm of N. B. Phelps and Company and began a course of training in business.

I doubt that young Clarke was a regular theatre-goer. But in January of 1870 Booth's new Hamlet, in the gorgeous theatre he had built only a year before, was the talk of the town. Long known for the beauty of his Hamlet, five years earlier Booth had laid special claim to the role in a record-breaking run of a hundred nights. All New York now welcomed the revival in its well-publicized new trappings. Clarke followed the crowd. He saw it first in its third week, on Wednesday, 18 January 1870.

He was overwhelmed by the experience. He had never imagined anything like this—Shakespeare so luxuriously brought to life, so handsomely mounted, so exciting at every turn, so thought-provoking, so perfect beyond belief in *Booth's acting*. He resolved to make a study of it.

In his leaderless youth Clarke needed a hero—a model to live by. His natural idealism, his aspiration to a life in art were half forgotten as he drifted into his fourth or fifth year at Phelps and Company. Then that one January evening the curtain rose on the hero he had unknowingly sought, Edwin Booth as Hamlet—ideal humanity realized in one person, beautiful in body, mind, and spirit—a model that he would memorize in the weeks and months to come and always live by.

But how should he go about it? Ironically, he took lessons from his business training. There is, after all, a certain beauty in rows of ledger books, in perfectly aligned columns of figures. He went at his problem decisively, in a businesslike manner. He memorized the play—that is to say, Booth's acting edition, which he purchased in the theatre lobby. He read all of Booth's current reviews and certain authoritative interpretations of the play by established critics. During the next nine weeks he saw the play *eight times,* taking notes constantly and refining them after each performance. He though earnestly about what the play and Hamlet and the actor meant and what they did for him.

Abandoning Phelps and Company, and the City, too, he moved to his brother's farm near Rochester, New York, where he spent the summer putting together in a large journal book a polished version of his great experience.

At the end of it, almost as if he were reviewing the profits of an investment, he summed up what the effort had been worth. "I never had a study that I enjoyed more than the study of Booth's Hamlet—never one that repaid me better for the time and attention bestowed.... It increased my faculty of judging character, my power of appreciating art, my understanding of Shakespeare, my understanding of myself."

In the autumn of 1870 he enrolled in the Rochester Free Academy, presumably to renew his literary interests, his efforts to write. Three years later he took his degree. He married. And presently it appeared, in the words of his daughter Emma, "the task of earning a living for his family prevented him from carrying out his literary ambition."

As his family grew and writing did not pay, he realized that he must find a world that would use and reward his practical talents. He took his family to the Pacific Northwest, where for fifty-four years he found work in plenty—as a businessman, a man of affairs. He ran cattle in the plains near Spokane. He moved to Idaho, founded the town of Post Falls, became commissioner of Kootenai County. In 1893 he moved into Spokane, where he dealt in real estate, in a security company, and in a fruit company. For twenty years he operated the Bonded Adjustment Company of Spokane. He died there on the last day of 1940, his ninety-second birthday.

If he never saw Booth again, as is most likely, the lessons in ethics and esthetics that Booth and Hamlet taught him enriched his long life. And the practical lessons of Phelps and Company, after all, were what made that life possible.

It was unthinkable to me that so conscientiously detailed an account of Booth's greatest role should be inaccessible. In 1969 I was satisfied that Clarke's methodical, clean, reporting as edited and published might be the closest we could ever come to the presence of Edwin Booth's Hamlet. If I had known then what Dan Watermeier can tell us now, I should have attempted a considerably different book.

In mid-June 1981, Professor Watermeier sent me word that at Harvard he had come across a pack of manuscripts, being commentaries on Booth's acting (mainly Shakespearean)—the work of one Mary Isabella Stone (1850–1921)—taking in the early 1880s. Later that fall when he showed me samples of his transcriptions, I was as determined as he that these Stone commentaries be published.

By far the longest set of her notes was on Hamlet, which she had seen six times during as many years, and Watermeier was pleased to observe that whenever she noted major effects the correspondence with Clarke's notes was fairly consistent. But what startled and pleased us both was the fresh personal quality of her interpretation of what she saw and heard. Clarke, so firmly intent upon exactitude, was wary of "reading into" Booth's acting what perhaps Booth never intended.

Once, indeed, in describing the Graveyard scene Clarke almost apologizes that his "fancy puts wings upon Booth's tones," and that he catches from their echoes meanings which have not been expressed: "But I write as I think and feel." Booth's acting, he says, is such that each word and motion is, as it were, a "stereoscope through which some great glowing view of a grand emotion or a magnificent idea is for the instant placed before my eyes." When he considers all that Booth has done for him—to drill his mind, to put edge upon his sensibility, to instruct his emotions, to inform his imagination—his impulse is to reach up his arms and cry with longing and admiration and humility, "Oh Booth! Booth!" It is as if Booth's identity and power were in the air overhead, and he were looking up to them as to a source of mental health and light.

Such semi-apology or such adolescent confession would never have occurred to Mary Isabella Stone. When Clarke first saw Booth in 1870, or when he put the finishing touches to his record that summer, he was still a very naive young man. Miss Stone was twenty-nine when she first saw Booth and thirty-one in 1881 when she next saw him and began to write her impressions. She graduated from the Framingham Normal School in 1870 and served as "practice teacher" the following year. In short, though slightly younger than Clarke, she was out of college before Clarke even entered the Rochester Free Academy. When she first saw Booth in 1879 and 1881 she was roughly a decade older and more mature than Clarke had been in 1870 when he studied Booth and recorded the experience.

Her family background was evidently more sophisticated than Clarke's, of which little is known. Her father was a physician. Both parents occasionally attended plays with her. In the Stone household there were books to read and Miss Stone had leisure to read them.

Expectably her vocabulary is far more sophisticated than the "plain style" to which Clarke deliberately confined himself, and her whole rhetoric—her sentence-building, her thought processes—is more elaborate. Her description of Booth which Watermeier quotes at length is a masterly composition, moving in orderly fashion from top to toe—his overall stature, his head, face, voice, his power of concentration, his gestures, his beautiful legs (again and again she will refer to his graceful legs, in movement or at rest). In 1883, when for some reason he affected a more voluminous and decorated set of robes which concealed his legs, Turkish-type slippers with turned-up toes and—horrors of horrors!—a chestnut-colored wig in place of his natural full black hair, and—ye gods!—a *moustache,* which ruined his facial expression, she was outraged.

Being a woman, she was acutely aware of dress, and fills many paragraphs with the fabric, color, design, and decoration of costumes—soldiers in their armor, women's dresses in detail, and everything that Booth wore and how he wore it. Far from apologizing for "over-interpreting" what the actors never meant to express, she was a genius at seeing into and through the minds of the actors; however slight the tone of a word, the glance of an eye, the flicker of a finger, it wakened her imagination to perceive the love or fear or contempt or motive to act that which was unspoken. Her skill at expressing the "unexpressed" is brilliantly manifest in her treatment of "honest Iago" in a full set of notes which Professor Watermeier submits along with the major section on Hamlet.

Her longer paragraphs provide us the most pleasurable reading, but careful attention to her briefest notes reveals or modifies many dozens of points of thought or action that Clarke omitted or understood differently.

Since Miss Stone is describing a Hamlet ten and more years older than the one Clarke saw, she is unwittingly recording the effect of real life events, many of them disastrous, upon Booth's playing. Betrayed by false friends he had lost his theatre and was driven into bankruptcy. He suffered the labors of the road to recoup his losses. He was nearly killed in a carriage accident; out of this his left arm, badly broken and badly set, never recovered its full use. In 1882 he made a long postponed visit to London, where he met a barrage of hostile criticism. Henry Irving rescued him from that by an invitation to the Lyceum, where for a month they alternated Othello and Iago. But meanwhile his wife, Mary McVicker, a hysterical woman, went completely mad and died. To fulfill an old dream, in the spring of 1883 he toured Germany and Austria, to gratifying applause but considerable loss of money. At home in 1883–84, he found himself out-rivaled by Henry Irving, who chose that inauspicious time to make his first American tour.

Miss Stone, probably unaware of most of these and other troubles, does make us recognize, especially in 1883, that something had been disturbing his artistic judgment. She finds him restored, however, when she next saw him in 1884. We come to understand that he was no fixed, unchanging thing, like his statue in Gramercy Park. For better or worse, as he responded to the vicissitudes of aging, sometimes he fell into depression and considered retiring, but sometimes his sufferings deepened and enriched his understanding of Hamlet. To quote another observer, Hamlin Garland, who was first seeing Hamlet about 1885, Booth had become "the passive suffering center, the good man enduring."

In the long run the purpose of Dan Watermeier's study is to demonstrate that there were two Hamlets, not one, in the mature Booth, or two halves of his Hamlet. In my 1969 study, following my witness, Charles Clarke, I presented especially Booth's *masculine* Hamlet, physically beautiful, yes, but what young Clarke especially sought for and found was an intellectually brilliant, earnestly ethical, in every way admirable character and man—a model for the good life.

In Booth's makeup, however, as in most complete geniuses, there was a strong feminine element. He was aware of this himself and was ever on the alert, especially in Hamlet, not to let this element degenerate into *effeminacy.* In Hamlet, I am sure, he perfectly succeeded. There were a handful of critics of the day—the "cigar and whiskey boys" I call them, "the boys in the back room"—who, harking back to the Hamlets of Edwin Forrest's generation, despised Booth for his lack of burly machismo.

But Miss Stone, who must have been a warm, generous, sensitive, mature, loving woman of strong judgment, saw Booth through a woman's eyes, and in her affectionate writing presents us a Hamlet not *feminine* or *womanly,* but a Hamlet to be loved by any sensitive observer.

Thus we are grateful to Professor Watermeier, and congratulate him for his accomplishment in bringing to print Mary Isabella Stone's beautiful record of *her* Booth's Hamlet. His labors have been immense, and his concern for the reader most generous. As one will quickly discover, he has keyed every quotation to the year it was made, to lines of the Globe edition, to Clarke's comparable notes as I reported them in 1969, to the Booth-

Winter *Prompt Book* edition of 1878, to references in the Furness *Variorum,* and other relevant documents. From his impeccable scholarship which has been manifested in many other of his Booth studies we have profited once more.

Here then, for our fuller understanding and delight is the "other half" of Edwin Booth's Hamlet.

Charles H. Shattuck
Department of English
University of Illinois

Preface

Little is known about the Mary Isabella Stone who compiled these commentaries on Edwin Booth's performances. She was born in Framingham, Massachusetts, on 24 January 1850, the daughter of Henry Orne Stone (1818–1909), a physician who practiced in Framingham from about 1850 until his death, and Mary Baldwin Lowe (1817–1891). Mary Isabella graduated from the State Normal School in Framingham (now Framingham State College) in July 1870. She was appointed a "practice school teacher" at the Normal School in September 1870, but resigned at the end of the academic year. She never married. At the time of her death, on 28 September 1921, her address was 999 Worchester Road, Framingham, apparently a home for the aged.[1]

Her commentaries were donated to the Harvard Theatre Collection in 1968 by Leslie H. Levinson, a used-book dealer in Framingham, who in turn had acquired them in a parcel of books and papers bought from an antique dealer.[2] Catalogued in the Harvard Theatre Collection as MS thr 219*68 M-89, the Stone commentaries actually consist of three separate documents:

1. A Booth *Prompt Book* edition of *Hamlet*[3] (5th edition, 1881) interleaved with about 200 pages of holograph notes on Booth's Hamlet.

2. A Booth *Prompt Book* edition of *Othello* (1878) interleaved with about 100 pages of holograph notes on Booth's Iago.

---

1. Gardner Barlett, *Gregory Stone Genealogy: Ancestry and Descendents of Dean Gregory Stone of Cambridge, Mass., 1320–1917* (Boston: Stone Family Association, 1918), 355–56.; Letter from Sarah A. Phillips, Special Collections Librarian and Archivist, Whittemore Library, Framingham State College, 1 September 1981. Letters to other descendents of the Henry Stone family disclosed no further information.

2. Letter from Levinson, 2 September 1981.

3. Between December 1877 and November 1878, Booth and his friend the drama critic William Winter, who did most of the editing, published Booth's own acting versions of fifteen plays from his repertoire as the *Edwin Booth Prompt Books*. Each of these plays was first issued by Francis Hart and Co. in New York in uniform, grey paperbound

3. A small handmade "book," about 4" by 5 1/2", constructed of folded and sewn sheets of paper, containing several pages of holograph notes on both Booth's Othello and King Lear.

Stone undoubtedly made her notes both during and immediately after attending various performances by Booth in Boston in the early 1880s. She meticulously recorded the performances she attended—usually accompanied by her mother—inside the front covers of her *Hamlet* and *Othello* notebooks, although she may have omitted recording her attendance at some performances. (See note 8 in the Introduction.)

She records that she saw Booth's Hamlet at least a half-dozen times as follows: 1 November 1879 (matinee), Grand Opera House, New York; 13 March 1880 (matinee), Park Theatre, Boston; 17 and 31 December 1881 (matinees), Park Theatre; 24 November 1883 (matinee), Globe Theatre, Boston; 23 February 1884 (matinee), Globe Theatre. She saw his Hamlet the first time, she writes, for "enchantment"; the second time for "impressions and recollections"; the third time for "criticism"; and the fourth time for "comparison." She explains that the "first time she saw Booth hardly counted for criticism." By the third time she saw his Hamlet, as she writes:

> I was quite familiar with his presentation of the part and I went prepared to watch, criticize, and remember for annotation, and succeeded well; nevertheless, his masterly acting, so intense, so spirited, so powerful, so varied, swept me off my feet before the end of Act I, and I felt the same enchantment, the same intellectual intoxication, as if beholding him for the first time, only with keener enjoyment than ever before because of my familiarity with the play as acted by him. My memory of his acting after this third time was more vivid than ever, and a revelation of Hamlet's character was afforded which will cast a never-fading lustre over that noblest, most fascinating of Shakespeare's personages. At the same time the entrancing mystery of Hamlet seemed more than ever impressive, his sweetness and winning beauty, the sadness of his isolation, his heart-rending fate! Ah, me!

The bulk of her Hamlet notes thus seem drawn from her observations at the two matinees in 1881, while her annotations of Booth's 1883 and 1884 performances aim at noting differences, changes, or refinements to this earlier performance. Stone distinguishes these latter entries by marking the 1883 notes with a green pencil and the 1884 notes with a red pencil.

---

octavo volumes. These plays were intended to be sold in the theatre during Booth's performances. The text was printed on recto only, so that the left hand pages would be free for actors', prompters', or spectators'—like Mary Isabella Stone—annotations. The *Prompt Books* were reissued in various editions over the next few decades. See chapter 3, "The *Prompt Books*: 1877–1879," in Daniel J. Watermeier, ed., *Between Actor and Critic: Selected Letters of Edwin Booth and William Winter* (Princeton, N.J.: Princeton University Press, 1971), 84–131.

She saw Booth's Iago on at least four occasions: 13 March (evening) and 27 March (matinee) 1880 at the Park Theatre; 10 December 1881 (matinee) also at the Park Theatre; and 20 February 1884 (evening) at the Globe Theatre. As with her observations on Booth's Hamlet, she distinguishes her comments on his 1884 Iago by marking them with a number or "dot" in blue pencil. She also distinguishes the 1881 performance by often noting it as the "third time I see Booth."

Her Hamlet and Iago notes are essentially moment-by-moment, usually line-by-line, descriptions of Booth's gestures, facial expressions, pieces of business, movements, and vocal interpretations in these his two most celebrated Shakespearean roles. They include detailed descriptions of Booth's costumes and makeup, and some brief notes on scenery and special lighting effects. Stone also often gives her highly personal reaction to the effect of Booth's acting at key moments in his performances. Furthermore, while she was clearly concerned mainly, even solely, with Booth's performances, she also includes some observations on Isabella Pateman's 1881 performance as Ophelia and occasionally a few notes on the performances of other supporting actors as well.

She records that she saw Booth as King Lear and Othello only once, on 9 and 12 November 1883, respectively, at the Globe Theatre. Her "book" of notes on these performances was probably a "workbook" in which she jotted down some initial observations and ideas. She then probably intended to recopy these notes into the appropriate Booth *Prompt Book* editions at a later time, refining, reorganizing, and even perhaps expanding them as a result of additional observations. But, either because she lost interest or lacked additional opportunities, she never added to these notes.

Her commentaries on Othello describe Booth's costumes and, almost line-by-line, his vocal interpretation, gestures, facial expressions, and business, but for the last climactic scene only. They vividly evoke, however, Booth's performance in this scene. Her notebook on Booth's Lear contains only a few observations on the Lear-Poor Tom scene (III. 4. 46–190) and the "recognition scene" (IV. 7. 1–84). Indeed, she seems not to have intended to annotate this performance fully, but rather, as she herself writes, to describe only the "special parts" which were the "most touching," "vivid," or "electrical."[4]

It was not my intention to use Stone's commentaries to "reconstruct" Booth's Hamlet or Iago in an original narrative or "novelistic" fashion. In the light of the studies of Booth's performances of these roles cited in the Introduction, such an effort, indeed, would have been redundant. In the case of Othello and Lear,

---

4. In an era when women drama critics were a rarity, Stone's commentaries offer the only detailed feminine view of Booth's acting, a view that was probably representative of the many women, young and old, who flocked to Booth's performances, particularly his Hamlet, throughout his career. Preserved at the Hampden-Booth Theatre Library at The Players are dozens of notes to Booth from unknown women admirers—offers of marriage and assignations, as well as simple and sincere appreciations of his artistry—that attest to Booth's distaff popularity.

Stone's evidence was evocative, but too meager to warrant "reconstruction." Rather, I thought it more important to let Stone speak to us with her own voice. Through her eyes and ears and emotional responses, an imaginative reader, informed with some knowledge about playing Shakespeare, should have little difficulty seeing and feeling Booth's performances as Stone herself saw and felt them. I have presented, therefore, Stone's commentaries in their entirety with as little editorial interference as possible. Students of Booth's performances, of Shakespearean acting, and of nineteenth-century theatre in general may be grateful for this essentially "documentary" approach.

Stone keyed her observations to specific lines of Shakespeare's text by placing a number or a letter—sometimes "color coordinated"—next to both the line and the corresponding "commentary," written usually on a page opposite or on a page following the text. (See figs. 1 and 2.) I have generally followed this system, but without the corresponding numbers or letters or "color coordination." I should note, though, that her notes on Othello and King Lear omitted the corresponding text references. However, I have by inference, sometimes aided by a direction in one of Booth's prompt books, correlated her descriptions to what I believe with reasonable accuracy is the appropriate line of text. I have incorporated her notes on Booth's Othello performance into the commentary on his Iago at the appropriate places in V. 2. I have arranged her notes on Hamlet and Iago chronologically line-by-line, identifying notes subsequent to 1880 in the case of Iago and 1881 in the case of Hamlet with the appropriate date in brackets. Her notes on Booth's Lear have been included as an appendix.

Although it is out of date as a "standard edition," I have followed the text of the Globe edition (1864) mainly because (1) it was generally the basis for the Booth *Prompt Book* editions[5] and (2) it facilitates cross-referencing Stone's Hamlet notes to Shattuck's *The Hamlet of Edwin Booth,* which is also keyed to the Globe edition line numbers. The Globe text has been used exclusively except for descriptions of the locales for scenes and stage directions which have been drawn from the Booth *Prompt Book* editions of *Hamlet* and *Othello* because they, for the most part, reflect Booth's scenic preferences and they correspond to what Stone usually observed in performances. Act and scene references in the running heads to this book also correspond to the Globe edition.

Stone's writing is clear, concrete, and fluent; even in the haste of composition, it is relatively free of grammatical errors and misspellings. She does frequently omit articles and sometimes abbreviates—"&c." for "etc.," for example. I have "silently" regularized her abbreviations in accordance with modern practice, sometimes added articles and pronouns, and corrected her spelling. Her punctuation is often idiosyncratic. I have sometimes changed it, by adding a comma or a semicolon when necessary to clarify a sentence, phrase, or idea.

---

5. Booth, however, did not especially like the Globe edition, which he described in a letter to Winter as "mischievous" and "doubtful," but he was persuaded to follow it anyway, at least for spelling, punctuation, and sometimes word choice. See *Between Actor and Critic,* 95.

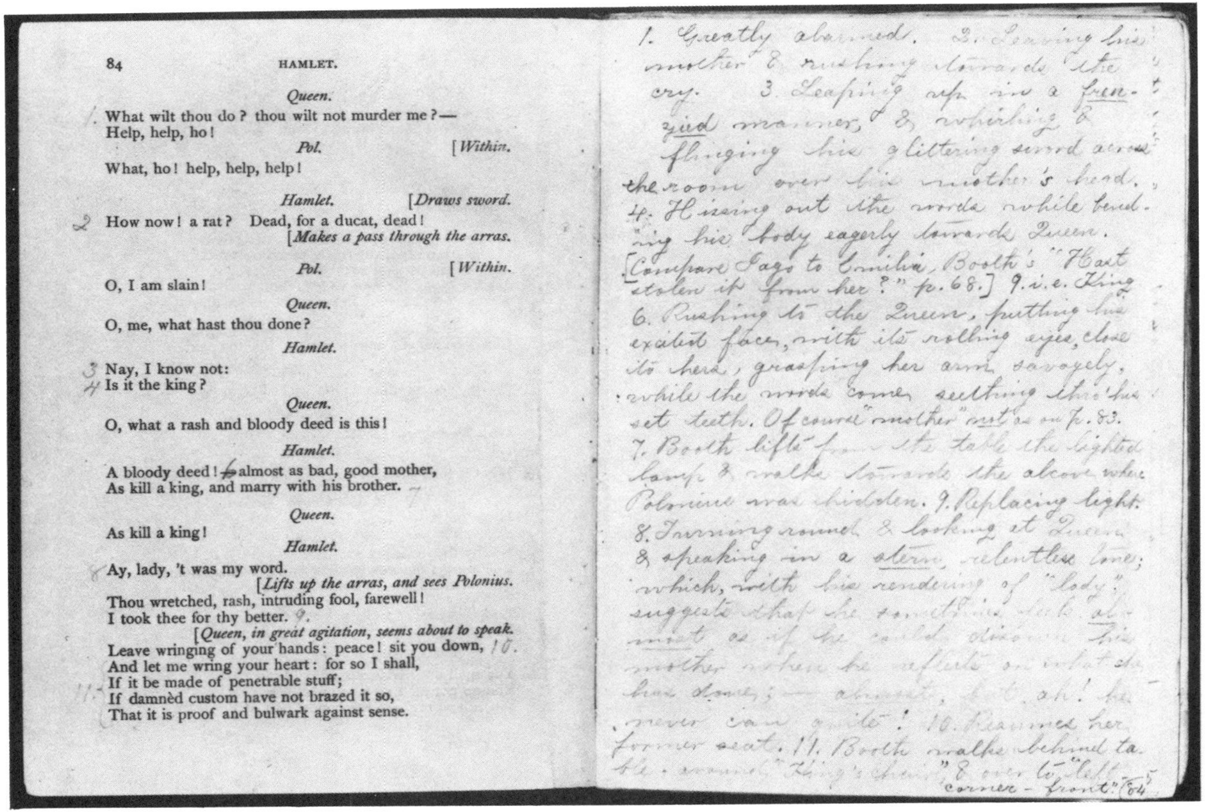

Figure 1. *Hamlet*, III.4.21–38
Manuscript page of Stone's commentaries.
(*Courtesy Harvard Theatre Collection*)

OTHELLO. 106

Emil.
My mistress here lies murdered in her bed.
O, are you come, Iago? you have done well,
That men must lay their murders on your neck.
Disprove this villain, if thou be'st a man:
He says thou toldst him that his wife was false:
I know thou didst not, thou 'rt not such a villain:
Speak, for my heart is full.

Iago.
I told him what I thought; and told no more
Than what he found himself was apt and true.

Emil.
But did you ever tell him she was false?

Iago.
I did.

Emil.
You told a lie; an odious, damned lie;
Upon my soul, a lie; a wicked lie:—
She false with Cassio!— did you say with Cassio?

Iago.
With Cassio, mistress.
What! are you mad? I charge you, get you home.

Emil.
Good gentlemen, let me have leave to speak:
'T is proper I obey him, but not now.—
Perchance, Iago, I will ne'er go home.

Oth.
O! O! O! [*At the bed.*

Emil.
Nay, lay thee down and roar;
For thou hast killed the sweetest innocent
That e'er did lift up eye.

Oth.
O, she was false! [*Rising.*
I scarce did know you, uncle: [*To Gratiano.*

Following the usual practice, I have bracketed any words, other than articles or pronouns, that I have added to her text. Occasionally Stone underlined a word in Shakespeare's text to indicate that Booth gave it special vocal emphasis, I have retained such underscorings wherever they occur.

I have annotated the commentaries as completely as I believe necessary for proper understanding without overburdening the reader with superfluous information. I have given, as one might expect, special attention to cross-referencing Stone's descriptions of Booth's Hamlet with Clarke's in the *The Hamlet of Edwin Booth* and often to Shattuck's own informative notes. In 1885 when H. H. Furness was preparing his *Variorum Othello*, he requested Booth to prepare him notes on his own performance of both Othello and Iago. More that 280 of these notes "For Ye Novice, H. H. F." are in the Furness Collection of the University of Pennsylvania. Furness printed most of them, and where pertinent I have referred to these as well as to those notes that he did not print. I also refer to several of Booth's extant *Othello* prompt books, relying most often on *Othello* #67, J. R. Pitman's very clear and full transcription of a Booth prompt book (or perhaps prompt books) made in the 1880s as a souvenir for the actor Russ Whytal. Since Booth autographed this prompt book, he presumably saw and approved it.[6]

I would suggest that readers wanting to make a close study of Booth's Hamlet and Iago as described by Stone should arm themselves with at least the following books: a Globe edition of Shakespeare's works with the 1864 line numbers;[7] *Prompt Book* editions (1878) of *Hamlet* and *Othello*; and Shattuck's *The Hamlet of Edwin Booth*. Surveying the essays cited in my Introduction, notes 1 and 9, will also provide excellent overviews of these performances and a context for understanding and appreciating Stone's achievement. Full bibliographic information on these and other supplemental sources can be found in the Selected Bibliography.

The Harvard Theatre Collection of Harvard College Library, which owns the Stone commentaries, has permitted me to publish them. Jeanne Newlin, Curator of the Harvard Theatre Collection, and her former assistant Martha Mahard on several occasions helped me in preparing this edition. Charles H. Shattuck, who introduced me to Edwin Booth's performances almost two decades ago, continues to encourage my research and with his usual generosity has furnished me over the years with numerous pieces of information and insights gleaned from his own studies of Booth and the history of Shakespeare on the American stage.

---

6. See *Othello* numbers 53, 55, 59, 65, 67–70, 74, 76–78, 90 in Charles H. Shattuck's *The Shakespeare Promptbooks: A Descriptive Catalogue* (London and Urbana: The University of Illinois Press, 1965). The notes to Furness are catalogued as *Othello* #76.

7. There are a number of reprints of this edition. Macmillan kept the revised 1911 Globe edition in print through the 1960s and in 1970 AMS Press issued a facsimile reprinting of the 1864 edition.

I am very grateful to Donna Fay Hall, without whose skill at word processing I would not have been able to complete this book. At various times Rebecca Blass and Margie Weaver also typed portions of the Stone manuscript. My friends Ron Engle and Felicia Londré have been steadfast in their belief in the merits of this edition. My wife Roberta Kane often lent her skills as a keen-eyed proofreader and critic. I take, however, sole responsibility for any remaining flaws in the text.

I remain indebted to the John Simon Guggenheim Memorial Foundation whose grant of a fellowship in 1980–81 funded my initial research for this book, as well as for several other completed and projected studies of Booth.

Introduction

Booth's Hamlet has been exhaustively reconstructed by Charles H. Shattuck in his splendid study, *The Hamlet of Edwin Booth.*[1] Shattuck's reconstruction is based on the Charles W. Clarke manuscript, which, like the Stone commentaries, is a very detailed scene-by-scene, line-by-line eyewitness account of Booth's 1870 Hamlet. Regrettably, the Stone commentaries were acquired only after Shattuck had completed his work; otherwise, I am certain they would have been used to complement, corroborate, and supplement Clarke's account. Stone's commentaries, however, are sufficiently unique and substantial to merit attention in their own right. Still, the two accounts are similar and different enough to invite some comparison.

Stone's commentaries, for example, document Booth's Hamlet more than a decade later than the Clarke record, during the period immediately before and after his important tours of Great Britain and Germany in the early 1880s. Booth was older, middle aged in fact, but at the very peak of his histrionic power and popularity. Stone's account is not as determinedly full as Clarke's, nor is it as "systematic." For example, unlike Clarke, she does not methodically record vocal accents, pauses, or variations in pitch, rhythm, or colorations. Like Clarke, Stone aimed to describe as concretely as possible what she saw and heard, but her observations are generally more personal and "impressionistic" and less "technical" than Clarke's. She writes that she wanted especially to capture Hamlet's "train of thought" (her expression), that complex web of feelings infusing Booth's characterization. Clarke saw Booth's Hamlet eight times between 18 January and 19 March 1870. His record is a composite account of these performances. Stone documents Booth's performance over several years, noting significant changes in business, costuming, and interpretation from year to year. As such, it is a "comparative" rather than a "composite" record.

Stone's Hamlet commentaries do not radically alter the image of Booth's Hamlet reconstructed for us by Shattuck after Clarke. It does, however, deepen,

---

1. See also John A. Mills's shorter but informative essay in *Hamlet on Stage: The Great Tradition* (Westport, Conn.: Greenwood Press, 1985), 125–52; and Robert Cohen, "Hamlet as Edwin Booth," *Theatre Survey* 10 (May 1969): 53–74.

enrich, and fine tune the vision. Stone, one might say, finishes the portrait of Booth's Hamlet begun by Clarke.

It is often, particularly when evoking Booth's physical appearance or visual effects, a very concrete portrait. Following, for example, is Stone's lengthy reaction to Booth's physique and voice in 1881. Booth was already in his late forties, but, for Stone, he was still like "a magnificent Greek statue" brought to life:

> Booth's stature is hardly above the medium, but his frame is so finely proportioned, well-knit, and rather slender withal, and his gait is so dignified, his entire mien so self-assured, firm, and graceful, that the effect of height is added. He looks every inch the noble Prince and true-born gentleman; strong, pure, and refined, in soul and senses. His symmetrical body is crowned by a finely-shaped head adorned with wavy black hair which clusters around a broad high forehead. His complexion is naturally pale and is unaltered for Hamlet. The face is one of impressive power and intellectual as well as sensuous beauty, with features cast in the rare classical mould; large, dark, deep-searching eyes, luminous, but not "snapping" or "sparkling"; the lips are thin, and beardless as well as the chin. To see this shapely head on broad shoulders; these handsome classical features, with a mobility of expression which is simply wonderful; this lithe and sinewy form;—why! it is like beholding some magnificent Greek statue suddenly endowed with life and motion, sense and speech, with soul, and moreover with the intellect and education of the 19th century! Let me not forget his white, beautifully shaped, yet muscular hand such as sculptors love to model:
>
> > Thou canst not wave thy hand in air
> > Nor dip thy paddle in the lake
> > But it carves the bow of beauty there,
> > And the ripples in rhymes the oars forsake.[2]
>
> All this, and more, to the sense of sight. But the ear as well as the eye is charmed and satisfied: Booth's articulation is refreshingly distinct always even to the smallest iota, yet it bears no appearance of labored effort, of "mouthing." His voice possesses great power, compass, and flexibility, and a peculiar melody which make his intonations, at times, exquisitely ravishing. His voice must be naturally penetrating, and he has acquired the rare art of projecting it into the auditorium without the apparent expenditure of force, so that when desirable he can carry on a conversation with another actor on the stage in the low tones natural to the occasion or their proximity, or even whisper etc. and yet make every word audible to the spectators. The timbre of his voice is not that of metallic clearness, of bell-like purity, instrumental musicalness, sometimes heard and admired; it is not a remarkably resonant voice. But it is rich and mellow and sufficiently strong. Its great charm lies in its marvellous modulations so perfectly adapted to the thought or emotion expressed.

It was not only Booth's physical appearance, or his voice, however, that impressed Stone. She recognized his "genius" as an actor and the metaphysical or spiritual dimension of his portrayal:

---

2. Ralph Waldo Emerson's "Rhythm," although Stone has substituted "hand" for "staff" in the original.

Hamlet seems a being of superior mould to any of those around him yet he has no apparent self-conceit; he is really of so much higher cast of mind, of so much larger soul, that is evident in all his words and actions. His intellect is so keen that it makes playthings of what puzzles others, and itself broods over problems of life, death, and eternity which few of his contemporaries cares to consider, even superficially.

Booth's immense superiority as an actor over all his companions, make this characteristic of Hamlet, of course, more conspicuous. Even Horatio, dear chosen friend of Hamlet, though he be, is far from being Hamlet's equal as man to man. Hamlet's isolation is pathetic. In the conflict between his conscience and his filial piety, he is so utterly alone; there is no one upon whose superior judgement he can rely. Horatio is willing to do anything he wishes, but he cannot tell him what he ought to wish, ought to do. Like a demi-god he moves among the lesser men around him.

Booth's gesticulation is frequent and less varied than his facial expressions. The latter, as a general thing, he employs more when other actors are speaking—the former during his utterances. Possibly a fault of his acting may be too frequent gesticulation; yet it is always most appropriate, and so graceful as to be rhythmic, poetical.

At all times and in all situations Booth seems utterly oblivious of the audience and conscious only of the stage and other actors. This even when some rare bit of his acting calls forth rapturous applause. This, of course, is as it should be. If on first entering the stage he (as is usually the case) be greeted by applause, he never notices it, as most actors do, by even a slight bow or smile, or conscious expression.

Though Booth greatly alters his tones and manners in different scenes to suit varying moods, yet throughout any one play, he is always the same person. But when he comes to act in another drama; it is immense and fundamental, radical: he seems as if actually another individual, more so than would seem possible. You may say "Of course," but I tell you it is by no means "Of course" except with an actor of genius. Never does he remind you during a play of one of his other characters. In one or two instances, careful reflection afterwards may suggest, in some gesture, or brief expression of countenance, that the same man was the actor in both cases. On the stage nothing betrays him but his voice, and this by its power, great flexibility, and vast compass; its tones are not the same. Sometimes he even extracts from it that subtle element of one's own personality (whereby we recognize our friends unseen) and as in "Richelieu" assumes and sustains a complete "false voice."[3]

Notice that in all his varied and frequent changes of attitude, often while himself talking, Booth never allows said changes to take place so as to disturb his utterance, but makes them in a momentary pause between his words, so that you never lose hearing a word. At the same time, this is not apparent.

Notice particularily the striking and always appropriate differences of manner and tone assumed by Booth. When alone he can give free rein to his inmost thoughts and deepest emotions and when he cannot, as he says . . . "But break my heart,—for I must hold my tongue!" as friends or acquaintants enter.

---

3. Booth's most popular non-Shakespearean role was Cardinal Richelieu in Edward Bulwer's *Richelieu; or, The Conspiracy* (1839). As Richelieu, Booth sometimes assumed an old man's husky tremble. See Daniel J. Watermeier, "Edwin Booth's Richelieu," *Theatre History Studies* 1 (1981): 1–19. Stone records that she saw Booth as Richelieu on 17 March 1880.

Figure 3.   Booth in London, 1882
This photograph was taken of the actor in a cloak
decorated differently from the one he usually wore. The
pendant on the necklace is actually the medal Booth
received following his Hundred Nights *Hamlet* in 1864–65.
*(Courtesy of the Hampden-Booth Theatre Library at The
Players, New York City)*

Stone was, however, less rapturous about Booth's 1883 performance. As note after note discloses, it was for her an often very different, puzzling, and disappointing interpretation. Her negative response stemmed in part from Booth's new, "more youthful" makeup and costumes.

For example, in the first three acts in his 1880–81 performances, Booth wore a long, full, lusterless, plain black cloak, a Renaissance "scholar's gown." In 1883, however, she describes Booth wearing a different, fancier cloak in the opening scenes, made of "quilted black silk trimmed with black lace." This cloak was so large and long it swept the floor behind whenever he walked and when he sat it enveloped his entire body except his feet. Then in Act II, Booth appeared in a different long, black "student's gown" that was "loosely girdled around the waist with a dark blue sash, overshot with black lace." He wore this gown until the fencing match, except in the out-of-doors scenes when he switched to his usual black fur cloak. Stone reports that the gown hid Booth's "beautifully shaped legs" and detracted from "the gracefulness of his walk and standing attitudes" and "the art of sitting on the quaint arm chairs."[4] To these fancy gowns Booth also added "a small round, visorless black cap trimmed with jet" and "black pointed shoes or gaiters coming up considerably above the ankle in points."

Booth was a master at makeup, taking great pains to create a unique face for Macbeth, Lear, Othello, or Richelieu. But as Hamlet he always appeared *au naturel*. Even after he turned grey, he still scorned a more youthful looking wig for this role.[5] But in 1883, Booth wore a "long curly wig" of "auburn chestnut color" and "a faint mustache"! Futhermore, there was "considerable color in his cheeks, and indeed diffused over his entire face and neck."[6]

Stone thought "the wig both in shape and color, . . . very unbecoming, hiding as it were the fine shape of his head and neck, and the natural carriage of his head on his shoulders," while the moustache greatly weakened "the former noble expression of his mouth." To Stone, the effect of the "frightful" wig and makeup, particularly when combined with the fancy gown, cap, and pointed shoes, was "altogether hideous." She complained that the combination "so disguises my god-like Hamlet that disappointment and disgust half spoil my enjoyment."

She thought that this new Hamlet was in some respects "more youthful" in keeping with his new physical appearance, "attempting to shallow the character of his former Hamlet to suit this youth." He moved "more quickly," spoke "more lightly," gazed "less into the depths of an unseen world of brooding melan-

---

4. The "quaint arm chairs" are the X-shaped, late Medieval chairs which Booth used in several scenes.

5. Charles H. Shattuck, *The Hamlet of Edwin Booth* (London and Urbana: University of Illinois Press, 1969), 306–7.

6. The critic of the Boston *Herald* of 20 November 1883 also observed the new "shadow of a moustache" and "locks of a light brown hue." He also alluded to a new "skirted costume." Curiously none of the other major newspaper critics mention the new makeup or costume. It is also not reported by Shattuck.

choly." She wrote that she endorsed "in nearly every respect" the review of Booth's "new" Hamlet by Alice Browne in the *Boston Evening Transcript* of 24 November. Browne, like Stone, also observed that Booth's new Hamlet was essentially "a beautiful-natured youth." In this new interpretation, according to Browne, Booth's Hamlet was more "melodramatic" than "dramatic," more like the Hamlets of Salvini and Rossi,[7] more prone to action than to reflection, more open and impetuous, and with a more pronounced "devilish relish of humor."

Stone did not characterize Booth's new interpretation as melodramatic, but she did note that "it seems less reality, more acting":

> Booth does not take possession of my faculties and sway my heart and brain at the will of Hamlet. There is something mechanical about his acting throughout the play, a strange lack of the usual spiritual intensity of that glow from the soul outwards which made Booth seem the living, breathing Hamlet of Shakespeare himself, containing deeps of being more profound than any words he spoke! Now so far as he is Hamlet, it seems to be in virtue of an assumption of the part: something put on outside.

Both Browne and Stone clearly preferred Booth's old and older, more ambiguous and complex Hamlet. Still Stone conceded that this new Hamlet showed Booth's "great versatility." The defects were "discerned only by comparison of Booth with himself." Even his new Hamlet was "finer no doubt, considered absolutely, than any other on the present stage." Browne also conceded that no other actor could "play two Hamlets of such fineness."

What were Booth's reasons for these changes? Browne suggested that it was a "self-defense" against encroaching age (Booth was 50) and/or that it was the result of Booth's recent playing to foreign audiences "who must depend on the action rather than the word." As a result of this experience, he had "sacrificed fine shades of meaning to telling ones, and thrown a stronger light on the springs of action."

Stone, however, was not totally satisfied with Browne's explanations. She believed this new Hamlet was a deliberate attempt by Booth to modify his style and interpretation:

> Booth's delivery of his sentences, especially in conversation, is less elaborate and emphatic, he makes fewer telling "points" with his voice; but I noticed the same change in his "Richelieu" in 1883,[8] and I think it may be attributed to a set purpose

---

7. Tommaso Salvini (1829–1915), Italian actor-manager, more acclaimed for his Othello than his Hamlet, made five tours of the United States. On several occasions in 1886, Booth played Iago to Salvini's Othello. Ernesto Rossi (1827–1896), Italian actor-manager, toured the United States in 1881–82 appearing in several Shakespearean roles, including Hamlet. See Marvin Carlson, *The Italian Shakespearians* (Washington, D.C.: Folger Shakespeare Library, 1985), especially chapters 6 and 7 on the Hamlets of Salvini and Rossi, respectively,

8. Her attendance at a *Richelieu* performance in 1883 is unrecorded.

on his part not only to eliminate from his acting the last traces of "staginess," but also to avoid any tendency to declamation, to fine elocution, a style not in accord with Nature. After all, it is very difficult to put one's finger on any portion of the play to state that here Booth acted differently, expressing this sentiment instead of that; yet quite unmistakeable is my consciousness of a decided difference in the personality of Hamlet throughout the play.

There were, moreover, certain inconsistencies if Booth wished solely to present a more youthful Hamlet. Stone noticed, for example, that Booth's acting in the interview with Ophelia tended to make more probable Claudius' remark: "Love! his affections do not in that way tend." This alteration, Stone noted, was not suited to the concept of a more youthful Hamlet. On the other hand his "lessening of sadness" in the graveyard scene agreed with the idea of a fresher, younger Hamlet. She concluded by remarking that, if indeed Booth was getting too old for Hamlet, then perhaps the other characters should be dressed and made up to appear even older than the text requires. Following such a scheme, Booth's Hamlet by contrast might appear younger than his actual years. In any case, she wrote, "Let everything feasible be done to postpone the lamentable day when Edwin Booth must forever lay aside the part of Hamlet as he has already done that of Romeo."

With what one imagines to be a sigh of relief, Stone observed that Booth's 1884 Hamlet had returned to an interpretation much closer, particularly in costuming and makeup, to his 1880–81 conception.

While the differences between Booth's 1883 performance and his performances in 1881 and 1884 are perhaps the most startling of Stone's revelations, there are numerous other occasions when Stone records a piece of business, a gesture, a movement, or an effect, for example, that is not recorded by Clarke, or is strikingly different from, or more detailed than Clarke's account. In every instance where this occurs, I have remarked on it in a footnote.

Although less extensive than her notes on Booth's Hamlet, Stone's commentaries on his Iago are the most detailed extant descriptions of his performance in this role. They substantially augment two earlier scholarly studies of Booth's Iago.[9] They were a primary source for my own 1986 essay; however, intending

---

9. Marvin Rosenberg has economically, but authoritatively, described the shape and impact of both Booth's Othello and Iago in *The Masks of Othello* (Berkeley: University of California Press, 1961), 80–88, 128–34; see also Arthur Colby Sprague's essay on Booth's Iago in *Shakespearian Players and Performances* (Cambridge: Harvard University Press, 1953), 121–209; Daniel J. Watermeier, "Edwin Booth's Iago," *Theatre History Studies* 6 (1986): 32–55; and Daniel J. Watermeier and Ron Engle, "Booth and Dawison's Polyglot *Othello*," *Theatre Research International* 13 (Spring 1988): 48–56. Rosenberg also reports on various moments in Booth's Lear in *The Masks of King Lear* (Berkeley: University of California Press, 1972). Two recent studies, *Othello*, edited by Julie Hankey, and *King Lear*, edited by J. S. Bratton, the first two volumes in a series entitled *Plays in Performance* issued by Bristol Classical Press, Bristol, England in 1987, provide extensive line-by-line comparative information on various

to be thorough but not definitive, I cited only about a third of Stone's Iago notes. As with Hamlet, Stone's Iago commentaries do not significantly change our received image of Booth's characterization, but they do graphically flesh out that image. Moreover, they also suggest in very concrete terms *how* Booth achieved—with an artistry that often concealed his art—his effects as Iago.

Again and again Stone reveals herself to have been an exceptionally acute, articulate, thoughtful student of theatrical performance. Ultimately what her commentaries reveal is that the greatness of Booth's performances (or for that matter the performance of any great actor) lay not so much in his arrangement of the text, nor in the appropriateness of his physique and temperament to the role, nor in his conception of the character, but rather, perhaps principally, in his orchestration of text, concept, appearance, and temperament with the physical imagery of gestures, movements, and vocal delivery. It is in their preservation of this physical imagery and its effect of one admiring but undoubtedly representative spectator that Stone's commentaries are especially valuable.

---

performances of the major roles from the eighteenth century to the present day. The *Othello* volume includes a fair amount of information on Booth's performances. The *Lear* volume contains little on Booth, although it does include a rare photograph of Booth as Lear.

Booth's Hamlet

Figure 4.   Oliver Lay, *Edwin Booth as Hamlet,* 1887
Oil on canvas.
(Photograph courtesy of History of Art Department,
University of Warwick. From the RSC Collection,
Stratford-upon-Avon, England, with the permission of the
governors of the Royal Shakespeare Theatre)

Act I

Scene 1

Elsinore. A Platform before the Castle. Moonlight[1]

[Globe edition I.1. 175 lines cut to 104]

Soldiers are dressed in glittering armor of steel plated mail with gray sleeves and leggings, helmets, tall halberds, etc. Marcellus is distinguished by scarlet sleeves and scarlet trappings on his legs, and by a gilded hoop arching over top of his helmet; his armor is also more elaborately wrought. He must be an officer of rank in the army. Witness, also, in future scenes he stands guard in palace, and has access to King and Queen, especially [in IV.2].

A silent tableau, lasting for at least one minute, before Bernardo enters at beginning of this scene, would make it far more impressive than the way it is always acted by opening the dialogue <u>at once</u> on raising the curtain.

Horatio is light-complexioned, fair, auburn or yellow, hair—a good foil to Booth. Horatio is dressed in a grey suit embroidered with black, a long cloak of same, and a cap to match; deep "turned-over" linen collar and cuffs.

---

1. Since Hamlet does not appear in I.1 Stone's comments, like Clarke's, are meager, confined mainly to description of the *mise en scène,* particularly the costumes and lighting effects. According to Shattuck, Booth raised the curtain on this scene, following the "eighth stroke of the midnight bell" to discover Francisco walking across the stage. In the middle of his cross, he hears from within Bernardo calling "Who's there?" Stone implies, however, that for the performances she saw, the dialogue began "<u>at once</u> on raising the curtain." Moreover, she also indicates that the setting was dressed with a number of extra soldiers. Booth's Horatios usually were fair-haired, either naturally or bewigged, to provide a contrast to Booth himself who played Hamlet, with the exception noted already, in his own dark hair. See Shattuck, *The Hamlet of Edwin Booth* (London and Urbana: University of Illinois Press, 1969), 74 and 115–18 for a description of the setting for this scene at Booth's Theatre in 1870. All subsequent Shattuck citations refer to page, not line, numbers.

127. "I'll cross it, though it blast me."

He crosses the path of Ghost right in front of it.

158–64. "Some say that... is that time."

Spoken by Marcellus in Shakespeare's text.[2]

166. "But look the morn in russet mantle clad ... "

A gradual change from starlight to reddish dawn is perceptible on the stage.

Scene 2

Elsinore. A Room of State in the Castle[3]

[Globe edition: I.2. 258 lines cut to 210]

Enter the King, Queen, Polonius, Laertes, lords, and attendants.

Polonius and Laertes stand on right. King and Queen in middle of stage, Queen towards left. King and Queen enter hand-in-hand. In Shakespeare's text Hamlet enters with the others, which is far less impressive. The time of this scene is the day following Scene 1 and in the afternoon.

Booth is dressed throughout the play in deep mourning, in a suit of lustreless, soft, black cloth: a long tunic, tight fitting "small clothes"; even his shoes are of soft black cloth. Legs up to tunic laced with narrow black satin ribbon. Sleeves are ribbed with purple halfway up; narrow purple belt with end of purple tassels, to which is attached his sword, like my photograph of him. White quilted ruching at neck and wrists. His tunic is slightly trimmed with purple, embroidered with black. On ring finger of left hand, an emerald set in diamonds. In this scene he wears a long, <u>full</u> cloak of

---

2. Booth assigned these lines to Horatio.

3. In Booth's 1870 production this first Court scene was played, because of the "rise and sink" system of scene change at Booth's Theatre, without thrones: the characters entered following the scene change and stood. Obviously this was the arrangement that Stone observed in 1881 and it was the practice preferred by Booth. All extant prompt book records of Booth's later stagings reveal, however, as Stone observed in 1883, that this scene was "discovered" with the King and Queen seated on raised thrones. As Shattuck notes (122), the "presence of raised thrones in these later stagings of course altered and enriched the stage picture and movement." These two different staging arrangements should be kept in mind when reading Stone's commentaries below.

lustreless, smooth, black cloth falling in graceful folds from his neck, a hood (not up) lined with purple; cloak is lined with purple embroidered with black like tunic, and one end is thrown up wrong side out across his breast, so as to leave left arm exposed and free nearly to shoulder. The purple is very dark and less prominent than one might suppose. A black bag for pocket hangs from his belt.

[1883] On rising of curtain the whole court is discovered assembled. King and Queen seated on throne center back, lords, ladies and attendants standing around. Polonius at extreme left front corner, Laertes nearer King who sits toward left. Hamlet is seated towards right, but near the throne and lower than the sovereigns. He is dressed very differently as follows: a long curly wig of auburn chestnut color and a faint moustache! Considerable color in his cheeks, and indeed diffused over his entire face and neck. Set on the back of his head is a small round visorless black cap trimmed with jet. He wears a very large, long cloak of quilted black silk trimmed with dark blue, overshot with black lace. This cloak is so long that it sweeps the floor behind when he walks; and when he sits covers his entire body except his feet. Black pointed shoes or gaiters coming up considerably above the ankle in points. This cloak has no hood. The ruching and the ring are the same.

He looks moody, not to say even sulky. His discontent, and dislike for the King are much more evident than his sorrow for the death of his father. The wig both in shape and color is very unbecoming, and hides the fine shape of his head and neck, and the natural carriage of his head on his shoulders. The mustache greatly weakens the former noble expression of his mouth.

[1884] Dress same except that now his wig is black and not so long, and is nicely curled, and he has no moustache, so that he looks much nobler and handsomer. By the end of the first soliloquy it is evident that he is in better spirits, that he is playing with all his former force and fire and with increased art, if possible. He takes possession of me as of old! The tunic under his cloak is occasionally visible, and is trimmed with long fine black silk fringes.

64. "But now, my cousin Hamlet, and my son,—"

[1883] Booth rises and walks off towards right front corner. [In the next few lines] positions etc. are nearly the same as before; his manner is more stern and as above described; he does not look so handsome, noble, sweet, and melancholy, so truly pleasant and lovely as usual.

Figure 5.   Photograph of Booth
This black, hooded cloak was the costume he usually wore
for Hamlet.
*(Courtesy of the Hampden-Booth Theatre Library at
The Players, New York City)*

67. "Not so, my lord; I am too much i' the sun."

[1883] Booth looks sort of over his left shoulder at King.

[1884] The idea is conveyed to me that the King is "the sun" and that Hamlet is obliged to see too much of him.

68. "Good Hamlet, cast thy nighted color off..."

[1883] The King, Polonius, and Laertes retire leaving Hamlet and his mother on stage right.[4]

74. "Ay, madam, it is common."

[1884] Folds his arms.[5]

75. "Why seems it so particular with thee?"

The Queen and Hamlet stand in the middle of stage, Hamlet towards right, both face partially towards each other and partially towards audience.

76. "Seems, madam! nay, it is; I know not 'seems.'"

[1884] Stepping quickly towards Queen as if awakened to a desire to contradict her.

77. "'Tis not alone my inky cloak, good mother..."

[1884] Slightly handling his cloak.

85. "But I have that within which passeth show..."

Pressing his hand against his heart at "within."

86. "These but the trappings and the suits of woe."[6]

---

4. In the *Prompt Book* edition "The King, Polonius, and Laertes retire R." following 67.

5. Clarke does not describe such a gesture. See Shattuck, 126.

6. At this line in the *Prompt Book* edition, Laertes exited "leaving the King and Polonius. The King advances."

Walking slowly past footlights towards left front corner, then turning, he fronts the King advancing, so that the left side of his face is seen by the audience.

[1883] Booth remains at right of stage facing left and towards the "advancing King."

87. "'Tis sweet and commendable in your nature, Hamlet..."

Hamlet's dislike of King is quite perceptible, a cold politeness, and always an avoidance of speaking to him except when obliged to answer a question. Booth stands left front with back partly to audience and facing King and Queen who stand in middle of stage, Queen nearest Hamlet. Side view is presented of Booth's face part of the time.

Booth's manner is of gentle, subdued sadness, expressive of the natural grief of a fond son at the death of an adored father. His eyes are bent upon the ground, even as his mother bids him not to do so, [70. "Do not for ever with thy vailed lids ... "] and only when spoken to does he raise his head. A certain indefinable languor surrounds him, an indifference as to what may become of himself, as to "all the uses of this world." He generally does not heed his companions, unless forced to do so by their address.

108. "As of a father ... for let the world take note..."

[1883] Booth shrugs his shoulders and expresses aversion (aside).

117. "Our chiefest courtier, cousin, and our son."

[1884] Booth bows slightly to the King, a mere form of politeness.

120. "I shall in all my best obey you, madam."

Bowing to his mother slightly, with respectful deference, Booth does not emphasize the "you" specially (as does Fechter) but rather the "obey"; yet by his manner he conveys plainly the idea that he consents to stay solely because she desires it.[7] You feel sure that nothing the King has said, or

---

7. The Anglo-French actor Charles Albert Fechter (1824–79) made his American debut in New York in January 1870 and remained in the United States until his death. Many critics praised his Hamlet as fresh and "naturalistic"; others decried its unconventional idiosyncracies. Stone could have seen his Hamlet in either New York or Boston

could say would weigh a feather in the balance with regard to any of Hamlet's actions.

Following 128. March. Exeunt all except Hamlet.

Booth walks after the retiring court and stands at the center back entrance looking after them, and you fancy he sees mutual expressions of affection pass between the King and Queen unseen by the audience.

129. "O, that this too too solid flesh would melt . . ."

In this famous soliloquy is disclosed not only a bereaved heart but one whose own consistency and vereration for a father has been wounded and outraged by his mother's lack of fidelity and "O'er hasty marriage" with her husband's brother, a mean man whom Hamlet always despised as worthless. Most edifying is it to contrast one's recollection of Booth's rendering of this with that of the other renowned soliloquies.

[1884] Booth walks over to the throne dais, carpeted in crimson, and puts one foot up on the lowest step; so his leg with its tight, black long stocking comes out from the folds of cloak and shows gracefully; he looks after the retreating court.

133. "How weary, stale, flat and unprofitable . . ."

Clasping his hands and hanging down his arms in front of himself.

141. "That he might not beteem the winds of heaven . . ."

---

where Fechter appeared in December-January, 1870–71. John Mills, in his "The Modesty of Nature: Charles Fechter's Hamlet," *Theatre Survey* 15 (May 1974): 59–78, cites this line reading as an example of Fechter's novel approach to the interpretation of Shakespeare's text. Of course, the line should be scanned with the emphasis on "obey" rather than "you." But Fechter seems frequently to have employed such irregular, "naturalistic" readings to create "a fully credible image of 'a living human being.'" While Booth had a similar objective, his line readings were generally much more regular. While Stone obviously had seen Fechter's Hamlet (see below, page 24), she does not seem to have been particularly struck by his interpretation. Booth had seen Fechter's Othello in London in 1861 and disliked it; but he nevertheless tried to contract him for an engagement at Booth's Theatre in the fall of 1870. Whether Booth ever saw Fechter's Hamlet is not known—probably not—although his curious 1883 interpretation described by Stone does suggest some Fechterian traits. The "standard" biography of Fechter is Kate Field's *Charles Albert Fechter* (New York, 1882).

Looking out into lobby as if recalling how the King and Queen looked going out just now.

[1884] Laying his clasped hands upon his breast.

142–43. "Heaven and earth!/Must I remember?"

Moving away from his station hitherto at the side of the center entrance and walking over to the left.

146. "Let me not think on't—Frailty thy name is woman!—"

Spoken standing at left, facing right with hand striking forehead, in an impressive way, which invariably calls forth applause.[8] Crossing stage to right [at the end of the line]. There is none of his subsequent, rapid rushing strides now; not great present excitement, but sorrowful reminiscence is expressed. There is a long pause.

153. "Than I to Hercules: within a month . . ."

[1884] Touching his breast and then brushing his arm aloft with pointed finger as if to express something immensely loftier.

159. "But break, my heart; for I must hold my tongue."

Pressing hand against heart, or rather grasping concussively his tunic at the breast.

At time of its delivery, this soliloquy seems to be rendered by Booth with adequate force and expression, and so it is. But comparing it with the volcanic outbursts of some of his subsequent speeches, one realizes how carefully Booth holds himself within bounds here. The sense of bereavement, of grief, shame, and outrage, that longs for refuge in the grave, all are well expressed, are sincerely, fully felt by Booth. But when by-and-by to these sentiments are added the emotions of supernatural terror, the horror and the agony of the Ghost's revelations and injunctions, the tremendous burden of the destiny to which he is called and the intense excitement which accompanies all this, then is revealed the transcendent genuis of Edwin Booth, and then is revealed, in backward reflection, the equally

---

8. Clarke does not describe this gesture. See Shattuck, 128–29.

admirable art of the opening scenes. About Booth's acting there is a smoothness, a temperance, a sustained strength, a magnetic personality, a sense of great "reserve power," even in the most exciting scenes. You never feel apprehensive of his breaking down in any respect, nor as if the force of expression had exhausted the fount of inspiration. He is like Samuel Johnson in this particular, not like Mr. Spaulding![9] From the very moment of his first entrance, Booth takes possession of the stage and holds if throughout the play, rising ever to the grandeur of the occasion, and presenting a thoroughly consistent, harmonious Hamlet. His interpretation comes from a soul on fire with genius capable by no means of writing the play, but certainly of appreciating it, and of developing and wielding an art which shall perfectly express that appreciation and so "when Shakespeare rouses himself and puts his glory on," I think in spite of Col. Higginson, that "the heights and depths" do "find an echo." You feel that the man Hamlet is greater than all he says or does.

Following 159. Enter Horatio, Marcellus and Bernardo C.

On entering, Marcellus and Bernardo step toward left and stand near center entrances and close together. Horatio goes towards right as he enters.

From their words of greeting and especially at [165. "And what make you from Wittenberg, Horatio?"] it would seem that Horatio had arrived recently and Hamlet had not before seen him to speak with him. But Horatio says [176. "My lord, I came to see your father's funeral"] which was over a month past.

Note the difference of Booth's manner towards Horatio and the other two; to the former free and friendly and hearty; to the latter, courteous to utmost degree, but formal without stiffness.

As Mother remarked, Booth has no need to tell Horatio in words of reiteration that he "is welcome"; his manner and tones express it and the intimacy between them made a confidence of welcome in Horatio's heart, and this Booth knows. Morever, Booth addresses them [Marcellus and Bernardo] as if he may have seen them within a day or two; Horatio not.

---

9. Possibly Elbridge Gerry Spaulding (1809–97) a congressman from 1859–63. "Col. Higginson" is possibly Thomas Wentworth Higginson (1823–1911), a Unitarian minister, supporter of women's suffrage, biographer of Margaret Fuller and editor of Emily Dickinson. Compare Stone's description to Clarke's as recorded in Shattuck, 129.

160. "I am glad to see you well..."

In Shakespeare's text this is said by Hamlet.[10]

As they enter, Booth turns around to see who is coming in; his station was near middle of stage facing left front corner.

161. "Horatio,—or I do forget myself."

Tone of pleased surprise. Shaking hands with Horatio while facing towards right end of stage.

[1884] Shaking hands with Horatio while facing towards left of stage.

163. "Sir, my good friend; I'll change that name with you..."

Still holding his hand. Emphasizing "that name."

165. "And what make you from Wittenberg, Horatio?"

[1884] Drops Horatio's hand, passes behind him, or at least Horatio's body hides Booth for an instant.

165. "Marcellus?"

Turning around to Marcellus waving hands and bowing courteously and slightly advancing but not shaking hands.

166. "I am very glad to see you."

Addresses Marcellus.

166. "Good even, sir."

Addresses Bernardo and in a more formal manner.

168. "But what, in faith, make you from Wittenberg?"

Putting his right hand on Horatio's left shoulder and looking him in the face.

---

10. After 1878, Booth assigned this line to Horatio. See Shattuck, 130n.22.

171. "Nor shall you do my ear that violence..."

With his left hand tapping or patting Horatio on the breast in Booth's peculiar manner of gentle familiarity.

174. "But what is your affair in Elsinore?"

Folding his arms and standing a little aloof and facing Horatio.

175. "We'll teach you to drink deep ere you depart."

Nodding and looking <u>rather</u> roguish and speaking in a hospitable tone.

177. "I pray thee do not mock me, fellow student..."

With Booth's peculiar shrug of the shoulders and sudden slight start. Putting his face close to Horatio's and his hand on his shoulder, but always facing audience.

178. "I think it was to see my mother's wedding."

Turning slightly from Horatio.

180. "Thrift, thrift, Horatio. The funeral baked meats..."

Shaking out both hands in front of himself.

182. "Would I had met my dearest foe in heaven..."

Gesticulating with clenched fist.

184. "My father!—methinks I see my father."

Gazing into vacancy with those fathomless dark eyes of melancholy sweetness; yet not a "vacant stare"—O no! But as if what he saw he loved to look upon.

185. "Where, my lord?"

Spoken eagerly and as if Horatio thought Hamlet really beheld his father with his bodily eyes—naturally enough, since he had seen him thus—[i.e.,] his Ghost.

185. "In my mind's eye, Horatio."

A long pause. At first Hamlet scarcely hears Horatio's question, then he makes a queer deprecatory gesture with both hands, lifts eyebrows, looks as if he would say "What do you mean?" or "Pooh! pooh, of course you know what I mean." [Spoken] in a tone intended to reassure and sooth Horatio and with an expression of amusement, perhaps even a hint of slight inward disdain, but latter not so as to be apparent to Horatio. Touching his own temple.[11]

187. "He was a man, take him for all in all . . ."

Laying his right hand on the left shoulder of Horatio (who still stands at Booth's right side) but immediately removing it. At the same time his face lights up with a smile, his tone is hearty with filial admiration. After "man" quite a pause.

188. "I shall not look upon his like again."

Looking heavenward.

190. "Saw? who?"

The tone is devoid of any suspicion of Horatio's actual meaning, but is emphatic, coldly curious, and has a tinge of disdain at what he supposes to be Horatio's "mal-apropos" words. [189. "My lord, I think I saw him yester-night."]

[1884] Booth looks with surprise mixed with a sort of disdain at Horatio and then at the other two as if to say "What does he mean?" [or] "What unseemly jest is this?" Then looks back to Horatio and says "Saw who?" as described above.

191. "The king my father!"

Continuation of same tone, increasing in intensity of curiosity mingled with wonder; also he turns round so as to face Horatio.

195. "For God's love, let me hear."

---

11. Neither of the gestures are described by Clarke. See Shattuck, 131–32.

Starting forward with eyes gradually dilating, fully satisfied that Horatio has something of importance to communicate. Surprise, curiosity, wonder, grow to astonishment, alarm, consternation as Horatio tells.

199. "A figure like your father..."

[1884] Turning round so as to have back to audience but still looking toward Horatio, and extending both arms sidewise stretching his neck forward. As Horatio proceeds, Booth glances from him to the others and back again, starts, gesticulates, etc.[12]

206. "Stand dumb and speak not to him."

Bernardo and Marcellus bow profoundly, as if to confirm Horatio's words.

212. "But where was this?"

Standing in middle of stage with his back to audience, throwing out his hands from his sides, addressing all three at once, and impatiently while wonderingly; Booth is also in front of the others, nearer the footlights.

214. "Did you not speak to it?"

Advancing towards Horatio at right back, touching him on his right shoulder, and addressing him, thus showing his own face again to audience with a shocked, disordered look.

220. "'Tis very strange."

With head slightly bowed and finger at his parted lips, gazing at the ground; he trembles all over.

224. "Indeed, indeed, sirs, but this troubles me."

Walking down center with hands at head.

225. "Hold you the watch tonight?"

---

12. As Shattuck notes (132n.28) Booth favored this full back position and used it with increasing frequency at various moments in his performances.

Turning hastily and addressing Marcellus and Bernardo.

226. "Arm'd say you?"

Addressing Horatio.

228. "From top to toe?"

Walking up stage past Horatio towards center entrance. Between [220 and 224] Booth seems convinced that they have seen a ghost, but still seeks proof of who it was.

229. "Then saw you not his face?"

[Spoken] like Fechter—as if to mean that the Ghost being "armed from top to toes" and visor down "You did not see his face, then?" Turning around to Horatio, being near him at right back.[13]

231. "What, look'd he frowningly?"

In a tone of longing eagerness mingled with a little fear.

233. "Pale or red?"

A tinge of affection added.

235. "I would I had been there."

Clasping his hands.

237. "Very like, very like. Stay'd it long?"

Meaning "Very likely it would have." Walking down stage.

239. "Longer, longer."

---

13. According to Field (99), Fechter read this line as follows: "Doubting, not willing to believe without strong evidence, he gave the line, 'Then saw you not his face?' as if it read 'Then you did *not* see his face,' which seems reasonable from Horatio's answer 'O yes, my lord, he wore his beaver up.'"

Again walking up stage as at "From top to toe" [228].

240. "His beard was grizzled,—no?"

In a tone of incredulity, and as if pondering whether it could have been his father's spirit seeking a "test"; [then] turning round to Horatio as at "Then saw you not his face?" [229] and also stretching out his hands to him, and speaking in a piercing tone of eagerness, anxiety, even entreaty that Horatio will not, need not have to answer "yes."

[1883] All this intensity of action is omitted and the question asked in an ordinary tone.

242. "I will watch to-night..."

Striding up to Horatio with a look of conclusion that it most probably is his father's spirit, and a look of decision as to his own course, and laying his right hand on Horatio's own.

[1884. At end of Horatio's line 241. "A sable silver'd,"] Booth gives a gasp and seems to gulp down a soul full of emotion, and to struggle before he can speak steadily.

244. "If it assume my noble father's person..."

Gesticulation with clenched fist of left hand.

245. "I'll speak to it, though hell itself should gape..."

Throwing out left arm, trembling, with distended fingers towards ground, at which he looks with horror—dilated eyes—while his tone is guttural with the force of his determination; and the words follow each other rapidly. [From 244 to 246—"If it assume ..." to "... hold my peace."]

246. "I pray you all..."

By a gesture drawing the others nearer to him, while he in middle of stage faces audience; and removing hand from Horatio's arm.

251. "So, fare you well..."

Turning around with the air of courteously dismissing them.

253. "Our duty to your honor."

[Horatio] departing; Marcellus and Bernardo go out first.[14]

254. "Your loves, as mine to you: farewell . . ."

Following them to center entrance, and shaking hands with Horatio, for whom "as mine to you," I fancy, is chiefly meant.

255. "My father's spirit in <u>arms</u>! . . ."

Back to middle of stage with hasty strides, hands at head; a long pause after "spirit."

255. ". . . all is not well . . ."

Walking quickly towards left.

256. "I doubt some foul play: would the night were come!"

Lifting eyes and hands towards heaven and speaking emphatically.

257. "Till then sit still, my soul . . ."

Convulsive pressure of his hands on his heart.

258. "Though all the earth o'erwhelm them, to men's eyes."

A comprehensive gesture with outspread hands pointing downwards to indicate "all the earth."

Following 258. Exit Hamlet L.

Slightly theatrical "taking the stage" as he exits.

---

14.   Booth assigned this line to Horatio alone, rather than to "all" as in the Globe edition.

Scene 3

A Room in Polonius' House.[15]

[Globe edition I.3. 136 lines cut to 94]

Enter Laertes and Ophelia. C.[16]

Ophelia wears a cream-colored dress trimmed with fringe around the neck, which is cut low; sleeves very short. Long, loose, flowing robe, with an extensive train; not fastened down at waist behind but flowing from shoulders. Light hair in long wavy tresses, neatly arranged with jewels though loose and abundant. Throughout this scene, her deportment is exceedingly sweet and modest, and affectionate both to her brother and to her father; she shows great respect for the latter. They enter with arms around each other, and stand to converse at stage right in caressing attitudes facing each other. Throughout Ophelia seems but half-conscious of her real deep love for Hamlet and wholly inexpressive of it in words.

10. "No more but so?"

---

15. In the *Prompt Book* edition, as Shattuck notes (137n.32), this scene did not have a separate setting but was continued in the "Room of State." As Hamlet exited left, Laertes and Ophelia entered at center. Some later prompt books, however, indicate a separate shallow setting in the first grooves for this scene. Such a setting would have facilitated the removal of the throne and dais in I.2 in preparation for a return in I.4 to "The Platform." Since Stone does not indicate otherwise, in 1881 at least, this scene was undoubtedly played in the same setting as I.2. Note also that she comments only on the 1881 performance of this scene.

16. Booth's Ophelia (and Desdemona) in 1881 in Boston was Isabella Pateman (1843–1908), an English actress who came to America with her husband, the actor Robert Pateman (1841–1924). Robert Pateman played the First Gravedigger in 1881. The Patemans had been members of the Booth's Theatre company. They were also members of his company during his London and Provincial tour of 1882. Although Booth was generally disappointed by his supporting actresses, particularly his Ophelias from whom he seems to have expected, as Shattuck writes, nothing more than "the personification of pale and feeble-minded amiability," Bella Pateman was, like Helena Modjeska in 1889, one of the exceptions. The critic of the Boston *Transcript* (15 December 1881) called Pateman's Ophelia "a sweet creation; her lines were recited in a rhythmic purity and her action was modest and engaging." Certainly Stone was attracted to her Ophelia. See Shattuck, 139–40, for a brief description of Modjeska's Ophelia in this scene.

Spoken in a tone of wonderment if it be true what Laertes has just said.

46. "But, good my brother . . ."

Drawing away from him, and speaking in tones of earnest, sisterly admonition, in which there should have been more archness, I think. Miss Pateman's voice is very sweet, clear and bell-like, and strong and she always speaks with evident loudness, so as to make the audience hear easily. This sometimes mars her impersonation, because it seems unnatural to the situation, especially when two actors are close to each other and are not excited. Her rendering of Ophelia, on the whole, was excellent; especially in her madness.

Following 54. Enter Polonius R.

Polonius enters at left. During his long speech to Laertes, [55–81] which is made at stage left, Ophelia approaches, puts her hands around his staff, and then one hand on his shoulder, and listens attentively and in a manner betokening loving deference.[17]

81. "Farewell: my blessing season this in thee!"

Again placing his hand upon the head of Laertes.

82. "Most humbly do I take my leave, my lord."

Walking towards door at left front corner of stage without turning his back on Polonius, who bows to him.

84. "Farewell, Ophelia . . ."

Ophelia advances towards her brother.

85. "'Tis in my memory locked . . ."

---

17. The direction of entrances and exits could vary, obviously, from performance to performance. The Polonius in these various Boston productions annotated by Stone was David C. Anderson (1813–84). Booth had hired him in 1869 specifically to play Polonius and other old men, Brabantio, for example. Indeed, he had been called out of retirement in 1881 to play such roles in support of Booth.

Stretching out her arms and placing a hand on each of his arms and looking up into his face affectionately.

87. "Farewell."

Kissing Ophelia.

Following 87. Exit Laertes.

At left front corner.

88. "What is't, Ophelia, he hath said to you?"

Polonius is standing near middle of stage where he walked after [82] and listened as if <u>partly</u> overhearing their words to each other [84–86].

89. "So please you, something touching the Lord Hamlet."

In an embarrassed manner and advancing hesitantly and then stopping.

98. "What is between you? give me up the truth."

Approaching quite near her.

104. "I do not know, my lord, what I should think."

Twisting her hands nervously together and looking down.

110–11. "My lord, he hath importuned me with love/In <u>honorable</u> fashion."

Very earnestly and with an undertone of appeal to her father.

113–14. "And hath given countenance . . . holy vows of heaven."

Said very solemnly with eyes upraised to Heaven and clasped hands.

132–34. "I would not . . . the Lord Hamlet."

Ophelia's bosom heaves, she looks confounded and distressed—dismayed—yet as if she dared not dispute her father's commands. She turns away from him and wrings her hands.

135. "Look to't, I charge you..."

Polonius walks away toward door of exit at right.

135. "... come your ways."

Pausing looking back at her and making a sign with his staff, meaning not only "Come with me" but "See that you mind me!" also.

136. "I shall obey, my lord."

Ophelia hesitates, looks toward him, looks away; then with a bright, innocent smile, runs to him, and they walk out together, her head upon his shoulder, his left arm around her waist, while she says [this line] in a girlish tone of <u>cheerful</u>, almost glad, obedience.

Scene 4

The Platform.[18]

[Globe edition I.4. 91 lines cut to 60]

Enter Hamlet and Horatio, to Marcellus, who is on guard.

Both arm-in-arm from left at back of stage (as in the Grave Digger scene—only now both are walking rapidly). By entering with Horatio to Marcellus, Booth emphasizes Hamlet's special friendship with Horatio. Time [of this scene] = 24 hours after Scene 1.

Booth is dressed as before except that now his cloak is of elegant black fur with a pointed hood drawn over his head, and curiously shaped lapels down over his ears and against his cheeks—<u>very</u> becoming; a long full whole cloak. This fur cloak is either lined with purple or put on over the cloak worn in [Acts] I and II.

[1883] Booth is dressed as of old in this scene, though not so pale as usual. Welcome is the dear old Hamlet! In these scenes with the Ghost he <u>seems</u>, as well as looks like his usual Hamlet.

---

18. The setting is the same as that for I.1. See Shattuck, 140, for a brief description of the scenic arrangements.

1. "The air bites shrewdly; it is very cold."

Walking down center towards footlights, rubbing his hands.

3. "What hour now?"

Returning and drawing his cloak around him.

7. "What does this mean, my lord?"

Standing on right, Marcellus having changed to left.

8. "The King doth wake to-night ..."

Walking down middle of stage and turning to face Horatio. Speaking rather contemptuously of King.

13. "Ay, marry, is't ..."

Nodding.

15. "And to the manner born, it is a custom ..."

[1883] Approaching Horatio and laying a hand on his arm, so that Hamlet's attention appears engrossed with Horatio and what he is saying to him.

16. "More honor'd in the breach than in the observance."

[1883] Booth turns away from Horatio and starts as if to continue his walk down stage (which he checked at Horatio's last question) thus Booth's back is towards Ghost on its entrance.

39. "Angels and ministers of grace defend us!"

All three start and fall back near back left of stage. Booth throws off the hood of his cloak, and almost falls backward into the arms of the others who support him. Moonlight breaks out and shines directly on his deathly white, awe-struck, yet eager and excited face while he whispers glancing upward "Ministers etc." The shock and the growing horror, as he realizes the vision, so affect his physical frame that he is almost overcome, is sinking down, down, his limbs giving way, and he seems fainting; his arms are outstretched against the two others, while his hands grope about on their breasts and arms in an aimless, failing way, and his face grows whiter. Still the brave spirit struggles for mastery, and he continues to address the Ghost in a faint, tremulous, but woefully <u>earnest</u> voice, lifting his drooping head with a gasping sob, and staring excitedly at Ghost.

[1883] Marcellus retreats to left corner back and Horatio alone supports Hamlet.

45. "King, father, royal Dane: O, answer me!"

"Father" is spoken in a tone of yearning fondness, and Booth kneels as he says it.

57. "Say, why is this? wherefore? what should we do?"[19]

Stretching left hands towards Ghost.

[1883] Stretches left hand and arm towards Ghost.

63. "It will not speak; then will I follow it."

[1883] Starting partially up, but not fully erect.

64. "Why, what should be the fear?"

Spoken softly, almost in a whisper, as if overcome with the dreadful spectacle he is witnessing; yet with the inflection of absolute conviction; sinking again into the supporting arms [of Horatio and Marcellus].

68. "I'll follow it."

Making a great effort and leaning on [Horatio and Marcellus] he rises to his feet while trembling in every limb.

69–74. "What if it . . . you into madness?"

Spoken rapidly and vehemently.

---

19. Compare Stone's notes to Clarke's vivid description of lines 58–91 in Shattuck, 144–45.

79. "I'll follow thee."

[1883] Here he addresses the Ghost directly, and he bows his head in token of respect, and I think he kneels again?

[1884] No. He didn't kneel again.

80. "Hold off your hands."

Booth struggles to free himself [from the hold of Horatio and Marcellus].

84. "Unhand me, gentlemen."

Drawing his sword, and at [85. "By heaven . . ."] laying about him with it.

86. "Go on; I'll follow thee."

[1884] Booth kneels again in middle of stage and bows his head over his sword hilt in his hand; his position is at some little distance from the other two.

Following 86. Exeunt Ghost and Hamlet. Horatio and Marcellus follow slowly.

Alarmed, awe-striken, greatly agitated with news in a tremor, yet strong in spirit of obedience and lofty curiosity, and irresistibly impelled, Booth very slowly follows the slowly departing Ghost. Apparently the Ghost disappears almost from Hamlet's watching sight, and he shades his eyes with right hand, and peers anxiously into the distant darkness of the castle grounds to see where it goes.

Hearing Marcellus and Horatio starting to follow him, he shakes his right hand gently out behind him, palm towards them, to hinder them. Then raises in both hands hilt of sword as the cross of protection for himself, and to appease any possible evil intention of Ghost—whom he is not yet sure is his father. Face pale and lips parted, head bent forward.

Scene 5

A Grove adjoining the Castle.

[Globe edition I.5. 190 lines cut to 170]

Scene apparently in some part of the castle grounds, an avenue and trees like a park.[20]

Enter Ghost and Hamlet.

From stage right. Ghost first; Booth has sword in right hand while he waves.

1. "Where wilt thou lead me? Speak . . ."

Booth stands by a tree in middle of stage close to background drop scene, facing towards Ghost who stands left almost hidden in shadow of trees, while moon light falls on Booth's face. His cloak has become unfastened at throat and thrown off of his right arm.

1. "I'll go no further."

With bold determination.

4. "Alas, poor ghost!"

With inflection of sincere pity.

8. "What?"

Meaning "Bound to revenge what?" From [opening lines to line 8. "Where wilt thou lead me?" to "What?"] inclusive, Booth's tone indicates that while following [the Ghost] his mind had been employed in reflection, and that now he doubts who the Ghost is; he speaks to it <u>more</u> as to a stranger than at [29–31].

9. "I am thy father's spirit . . ."

Booth kneels before him, bowing head.

22. "List, list, O list!"

---

20. Shattuck notes (147n.48) that in most of Booth's later stagings after 1878 this scene was set in "Another part of the Platform," effected, perhaps, by simply lowering a drop depicting another view of the castle. In 1881, however, Stone indicates a setting more like that used in the Booth's Theatre production. For a description of that setting, see Shattuck, 147–48, and plate VII.

Booth rises slowly and only partially, lifting his head and giving attention; he bears his sword on his right hand, point into ground as if partially to support his frame, which trembles with awe, and quivers with excitement.

24. "O God!"[21]

His features are suffused with emotion expressive of the love and grief he did and does feel for his father.

26. "Murder!"

Starting to his feet with a look of wild astonishment and cloak begins to fall off his back. Booth also steps back. Cloak is slipping off Booth's left shoulder, hanging on to his left wrist only.

29. "Haste me to know't..."

Booth hastily starts forward a step or two as if ready and eager to do it now, and moving his sword as if ready to use it. Cloak drops entirely off on to the ground, quite unheeded by Hamlet.[22]

40. "O my prophetic soul!"

I.e., "Ah! I thought so!" Lifting his eyes heavenward.

41. "My uncle!"

Then stretching, as it were, his very body in eagerness of soul towards the Ghost, with a strange exultant look gleaming thro' his awe, horror, and grief, as if he said "You mean my uncle, he did it, did he not?!"

42–79. "Ay, that incestuous... imperfection on my head."[23]

Booth listens with utmost attentive eagerness.

---

21. Booth substituted "Heaven."

22. Compare this business with the cloak from the opening line to line 29 to Clarke's account in Shattuck (150n.51); see also line 191 below regarding retrieval of the cloak.

23. Booth cut a considerable amount of the Ghost's narrative 42–91. See Shattuck, 159, for a listing of these cuts.

80. "O, horrible! O, horrible! most horrible!"[24]

Dropping his head upon his breast in a despairing manner; then resuming his listening attitude, as Ghost resumes speaking.

86. "Against thy mother aught: leave her to heaven..."

Booth gives a peculiar recoil as if from a fresh blow upon a spot already wounded. A look of perplexed distress, and of shame mingle with the previous emotion mirrored in his countenance. He had not thought of his mother before, of her special connection possibly with the murder, etc. For the first time, after seeing the Ghost, his inward eye is turned upon his mother; ah! she will never look the same to him as she did before this night! Her hasty re-marriage was bad enough had Hamlet, elder, died a natural death—but now! O what?

88. "Fare thee well at once!"

[1884] Booth kneels again here and holds up before him the cross of his sword hilt, lifting his face towards Ghost with a piteous beseeching expression.

91. "Adieu, adieu..."

Booth, during the latter part of the Ghost's speech, has been bending forward, half kneeling, eager to catch every word, showing utmost attention, honor, and sympathy, and deference too, in every nerve and fiber and gesture. As Ghost finally disappears, he falls heavily upon the ground, utterly overcome, with a clash of the sword upon which he has been leaning.

[1883] It seemed to me, specially during latter part of interview with Ghost, that Booth made more prominent the awe, dread, horror produced upon him by the vision—the nervous shock, the physical effect on him, as it were, so that he can scarcely support his frame to listen to the end, showing in his face, drowning at last even the mental alarm and astonishment and the emotions of agony caused by the news brought by the Ghost.

[1884] Bowing his head and sinking lower and lower, until at [the exit of the Ghost, following 91] he falls over sidewise and rolls in a swoon flat on the ground. Not exactly a swoon, however, as he begins so soon to speak.

---

24. Following traditional stage practice, Booth had Hamlet speak this line.

92. *"O all you host of heaven!"*

[1883] Said while lying on ground after a long pause.

92. *"O earth! what else?"*

[1883] Beginning to pick himself up slowly and desperately, lifting his head.

93. *"And shall I couple hell?"*

[1883] Lifting up, leaning on his right hand.

93. *"O fie! Hold, hold, my heart . . ."*

[1883] Clutching breast with left hand.

94. *"And you, my sinews, grow not instant old . . ."*

[1883] Throwing out one foot so as to show the beautiful arch of his knee and leg (so supple) free from any cloak or gown now.

95. *"But bear me stiffly up."*

[1883] With a light spring rising to an erect posture.

97. *"In this distracted globe."*

Clasping his forehead with one hand.

102. *"And thy commandment all alone shall live . . ."*

Spreading his arms and lifting his hands towards heaven.

[1884] Throwing head back, raising his right hand heavenward and looking thither also, making a grandly beautiful gesture.

104. *". . . yes, by heaven!"*

Kneeling in middle of stage.

112. *"I have sworn't."*

Bowing his head solemly and kneeling down.

113. "Lord Hamlet,—"

Booth starts and gives a wild look, as there flashes over him the recollection of his connection with these two and what shall he say to them? How bear himself to others whom he must meet.

114. "So be it!"

Covering his eyes with his hand as if in tearful prayer.

[1883] Not as perceptible as before.

[1884] Covering his eyes with his right hand as if in tearful prayer and still kneeling. He takes out his handkerchief and wipes his eyes and seems to suppress a sob as he rises to his feet.

115. "Hillo, ho, ho, boy! Come, bird, come."[25]

Here occurs the first assumption of the so-called "craziness" of Hamlet. But this unnatural "mad" manner Booth makes to appear by no means involuntary on his part. He is deeply impressed by the visitation of the Ghost, his soul is roused to a higher pitch of solemn excitement and his heart is not so weak as to have been unbalanced by even so terrible a shock. He assumes this manner and such words to avoid telling the truth to Marcellus and Horatio, to put them off, get rid of them, till he can decide what to do, and when, and how. Afterwards, [when] he has told Horatio the truth, an ironi-

---

25. In some of her "general notes" on Booth's performances, Stone wrote: "The only time that his manner appears as if actual insanity might be upon him, is in the interview with his mother. At all other times, the madness is most evidently assumed, as he said he might 'put an antic disposition on.' In fact, as Booth plays the part, no auditor can believe that Hamlet was truly crazy; rather he makes such a supposition seem utterly absurd and untenable. Booth's interpretation of the character throughout seems the only possible correct one. He is, indeed, the ideal Hamlet—the noble Prince, and perfect gentleman; he does not act Hamlet, he is Hamlet! Indeed his so called assumptions of the crazy manner are so superficial that I almost wonder that they deceived anyone except stupid old Polonius, whose pre-conceived idea that Hamlet was crazy for love of his daughter, made him blind. Ophelia thinks him crazy he is so changed towards her; then [in III.1.95ff.] he speaks so harshly rudely, almost wildly. Compare his madness with the reality of Ophelia's! See also [I.2.129–59, 'O that this too, too solid flesh . . .'] where he seems almost mad with concealed anguish, with the pent-up horror about which he must not talk. Then [in II.1.552ff.] Booth seems near frenzy. Possibly also at [II.2.174ff. with Polonius]."

cal tinge to his tone conveys to me the conviction that Hamlet's true self
rises to control his words still; reason sits on her throne. Throughout this
scene, "with the very comment of thy soul," [III.2.84] observe Booth's face,
especially during his private interview with the Ghost. Behold Hamlet's
varying emotions written upon it with heart-rending vividness.

[1884] Turning he goes toward center back waving his handkerchief high
above his head as he speaks and going to meet the other two.

116. "How is't, my noble lord?"

Entering from right back, Booth advancing to meet them. Just before they
enter, he turns aside and wipes his eyes and gasps a sob.

*118, 119, 121, 122, and 123. "O, wonderful! ... No, you will reveal it ...
How say you then...? But you'll be secret?... There's ne'er a villain..."*

Said in a tone and manner indicating to the other two the intention of
confiding in his hearers whatever has occurred since their separation from
him. Booth's manner is flurried, like that of a man whose nerves have been
badly shaken; at the same time there is a tone of irony unlike any before
used by Booth in "Hamlet."

124. "But he's an arrant knave."

Walking away from them towards left front corner.

126. "Why, right, you are i' the right..."

Turning towards them again and standing at left front. In this speech the
peculiarity of Booth's assumption of "craziness" is marked; yet not for a
moment do you suspect it to be anything but feigned.

*131–32. "Such as it is;—and for my own poor part,/Look you, I'll go
pray."*

Retiring towards center back. There is a touching, sort of wild, yet re-
strained sadness in the way he speaks this.

134. "I am sorry they offend you..."

Looking back towards Horatio.

136–37. "Yes, by Saint Patrick ..."

Advancing suddenly towards Horatio and shaking his finger at him as he says "And much offense too" [137].

138. "It is an honest Ghost..."

Resuming his natural tone and manner of seriousness.

139–42. "For your desire to know what is between us... One poor request."

Booth stands in middle, facing audience, Marcellus on his right, Horatio on his left; he takes their hands, presses their palms together in his own and lifts all up in front of his breast, and addresses <u>both</u> of them markedly.[26]

147. "Upon my sword."

The sword is lying where it fell clattering to the ground when Hamlet sank down overcome [at 91]. Points to sword.

147–48. "We have sworn ..."

[1883] The sword is stuck in ground in middle of stage. Booth points to it standing behind it and speaks in an excited tone.

[1884] Booth walks over to where his sword lies and picks it up, turns and presents it to them at "Indeed, upon my sword, indeed," [148] holding it hilt up that they may swear upon the cross. Booth stands really in the middle of stage facing audience.

149. "Swear."

Even Booth starts violently at this, but afterwards only Marcellus and Horatio appear alarmed.

150. "Ah, ha, boy! say'st thou so?"

---

26. This business is significantly different from that observed by Clarke. At line 137, "Touching this vision," Marcellus, according to the *Prompt Book* edition, "advances quickly R.," thus bringing him to center with Hamlet and Horatio. See Shattuck, 155n.59.

[1884] Spoken in an undertone, rather slurred over; but in a tone expressive of gasping dread beneath an assumption of boldness, and withal a very excited manner, almost <u>wild</u>.

151–52. "Come on . . . Consent to swear."

Moving nearer right of stage carrying his sword; addressed to Marcellus and Horatio.

154 and 159. "Swear by my sword."

Here Booth throws his head back and upward and his face is lit with high resolve; at once follows ["sword"].

[1883] I notice this especially in 1883, but think Booth always did so.

[1884] He does not do so. He looks straight forward and then bows his head over the hilt.

155. "Swear."

[1884] Both starts backward. Horatio, being nearest middle of stage, which leaves him at quite a little distance from Hamlet. Marcellus is then farther towards right and on Horatio's right hand.

157. "Come hither, gentlemen."

Moving towards right corner.

[1884] All three stand at right corner front and Booth has back towards audience.

165. "And therefore as a stranger give it wecome."

Walking up close to Horatio and laying his left hand on Horatio's right shoulder.

167. "Than are dreamt of in your philosophy."

As if it were "our philosophy." [Lines 165–67] are addressed exclusively to Horatio and in a lower reflective tone.

168. "But come . . ."

Addressing both again in a louder, brighter tone with sword in his right hand held by the blade hilt up. He handles it carelessly while talking.

170–81. "How strange or odd ... need help you, / Swear."

Looking earnestly from one to the other and compelling their careful attention.

174. "With arms encumber'd thus ..."

Folding his arms still holding sword.

174. "... or this head shake ..."

Shaking his head and imitating their supposed tones in saying the quotations [lines 176–77].

180. "So grace and mercy ..."

Presenting the sword as before at "sword" [154 and 159]. All standing nearly in middle of stage.

181. "Swear."

Booth bows still lower, bending with the sword hilt, so as to be almost kneeling.

182. "Rest, rest, perturbed spirit!"

Spoken in a <u>very soft,</u> sweet, reverential tone, but most distinctly.

[1883] Inaudible!

[1884] Spoken in the old, clear, sweet, distinct tone of revererence, but standing, and very softly.

183. "So, gentlemen ..."

Rising. This word ["gentlemen"] he pronounces with singular accuracy, and in a way to bring out its full significance. Sheathing the sword.

184–87. "With all my love ... shall not lack."

Spoken cordially and gratefully, albeit sadly. Putting his right hand in arm of Marcellus, his left arm upon Horatio's, while himself fronts audience, and looking from one face to the other with friendly and pathetic eyes.

187. "Let us go in together…"

Removing his hands and turning around.

188. "And still your fingers on your lips, I pray."

Putting his fingers to his lips.

189. "The time is out of joint…"

Turning to audience again, and clasping his forehead in anguish of spirit.

[1884] I think Booth does not separate himself so entirely from them both as before, but keeps his left hand on Horatio's shoulder, while turning towards audience.

189–90. "O cursed spite… That ever I was born to set it right!"

Advancing to front of stage, looking heavenward, raising aloft his right arm and beautiful hand, while the word "born" swells out in clear, rich, mellow cadences, yet with bitter, passionate, regretful emphasis applied to the entire sentence. There is <u>no tinge</u> of petulance, but a world of longing, regret, and a far reaching comprehension of all the future consequences.

Following 191. "Nay, come, let's go together."

Resuming his ordinary manner, and taking the arm of Horatio who is on his right as he turns again away from the audience. All retire towards center back returning to the castle. Marcellus picks up Hamlet's black fur cloak and offers it to him; the latter receives it with a bow of princely courtesy, and begins to lift it up as if to put it on, thus bringing his rare handsome profile into relief against its blackness as the curtain slowly descends.[27]

---

27. See Shattuck, 158n.67, regarding the retrieval of the cloak.

Act II

A Room in the Palace.[1]

[Globe edition II.1 and 2. 120 lines cut to 33; 634 lines cut to 463; total 754 lines cut to 496][2]

In the middle of the stage is a table at either end of which is an armchair and in front of which is a lower chair without arms. Two or three other similar armchairs—all of that queer, antique, quaint style, without backs, sort of short lounges—are suitably scattered about the room. At left, right and center back are doorways hung with rings [i.e., curtains hung on rings]. The one at center back is very wide and opens on to the "lobby." The low chair above mentioned as standing in front of table, I call "Hamlet's chair."

[Globe edition II.2]

5. "Of Hamlet's transformation . . ."

Seating himself at end of table towards right to be hereafter known as the "King's chair." The one at opposite end of table towards left [to be here-after known as] the "Queen's chair."

---

1. The setting that Stone observed seems to have been similar to the "Hall of Arches" Booth used in his Winter Garden and 1870 Booth's Theatre productions. For these Boston productions, this "Room in the Palace" setting was used not only for Act II but also for Act III.1 as, indeed, even Booth had done at Booth's Theatre after 1873. See Shattuck, 160–61n.1, and plates VIII and XVIb.

2. In his stage version Booth combined II.1 and 2 and then cut much of Globe II.1. Only portions, for example, of the Ophelia-Polonius interview 74–119 were retained. Stone did not comment on this interview. Her record begins with the King's speech (Globe edition II.2.1–18).

26. "As fits a king's remembrance."

Seating herself in a chair at end of table towards stage left [i.e., the "Queen's chair"].

At 26–32. "Both your majesties . . . To be commanded."

[Rosencrantz and Guildenstern] bowing in a most obsequious and fawning manner. [Rosencrantz] dressed in elegant green velvet tunic trimmed with gold lace.

Following 37. Exeunt Rosencrantz, Guildenstern, and all the attendants.

At center back.

95. "More matter, with less art."

King and Queen both appear "bored" and impatient of Polonius's tedious harangue. They are seated at opposite ends of a table in the middle of room; Queen being towards stage left. Polonius stands near her.

152. "It may be, very likely."

Queen rises, handles some article on the table in an indifferent manner, and walks off in front of King and round to right.

168. "But look where sadly . . ."

Looking out at center back into lobby.

Following 170. Exit King and Queen.

At right where Ophelia afterwards goes.

Following 170. Enter Hamlet, C. reading.

Walking in and toward right of stage around the table setting in middle of room. Booth wears a different house-cloak from that in Act I. This one is shorter and smaller, the longest part hanging at his back almost to the bend of his knee. 'Tis of same black cloth lined with purple. It hangs in full graceful folds from his neck, has no hood, and is not festooned up in any way. It hangs off from his shoulders in front so as to display his form. Over it is thrown a large silver necklace to which is attached a locket containing a miniature of his father. This locket is thrust into his bosom. He wears no sword. A dagger in a black sheath chased with silver is stuck in the belt of his tunic. His dress displays his fine form and graceful limbs even better than the one in Act I.

[1883] Booth enters reading, glances furtively and quickly to his right and left, and on seeing Polonius an expression of annoyance crosses his face.

[1883] A long black gown (similar in cut to those Booth wears as Richelieu) which covers his entire form down to his feet both in front and at back, thus hiding his beautifully shaped legs, detracting much from the grace of his walk, of his standing attitudes, and the art of sitting on the quaint "Hamlet" arm-chairs. The gown is loosely girded arounds his waist with a dark blue sash overshot with black lace; it has no sleeves, and arm sizes are large and trimmed with silvery beading. His black bag for pocket handkerchief hangs outside the gown. His necklace is thrown over the gown and hangs far down his back. Somehow whenever he stands back to audience he looks crooked, as if one shoulder were higher than the other! This is presumably a "student's gown," but it is altogether hideous and with the chestnut wig full flowing on his neck making him "run his head out" unnaturally, so disguises my god-like Hamlet that disappointment and disgust half spoil my enjoyment! This gown is worn all the time until the fencing-bout of the last scene, when the familiar tunic is worn, as before; except in scenes out-of-doors when formerly he wears the black fur cloak which he still retains.

[1884] Somewhat improved; the gown is shorter and open on the right side so as to frequently show his leg, and, indeed when sitting down, both legs partially; and it does not seem to impede his motions this time.[3]

173. "Do you know me, my lord?"

Before answering, Booth pauses long and gazes curiously at Polonius.

174. "Excellent well; you are a fishmonger."

Standing in front of King's chair and opposite Polonius who is left.

---

3. The 1881 description coincides with two extant portraits of Booth as Hamlet: an 1870 watercolor by William Wallace Scott (now in the Harvard Theatre Collection and reproduced in Shattuck, plate XI) and Oliver Lay's painting completed in 1887 (now in the collection of the Royal Shakespeare Theatre, Stratford-upon-Avon, England. See fig. 4). Booth may have adopted the 1883 costume during his German tour in January–April 1883 and used it regularly through 1885. See Shattuck, 124–25.

175. "Not I, my lord."

[1883] Booth walked around the table towards left.

176. "Then I would you . . ."

Moving chair preparatory to sitting.

178. "Ay, sir, to be honest . . ."

Booth sits down in low chair in front of table [i.e., in "Hamlet's chair"].

[1883] Sits in Queen's chair.

[1884] Sits down in King's chair.

181. "For if the sun . . ."

A dreamy look, gazing in front of himself.

182. ". . . being a god kissing carrion,—"

[1884] Looking heavenward.

182. "Have you a daughter?"

A long pause [before the line] followed by an utter change of tone to eagerness.

185. ". . . but not as your daughter may concieve."

With a strange, momentary look of real serious apprehension, yet as at [181 above].

186. "Friend, look to 't."

Casting a quick furtive look at Polonius to see if the old man "swallows the bait," [and] is well deluded by him. [Then he] resumes his reading, turning somewhat away from Polonius as if desirous of reading without interruption, right elbow on table.

[1884] Puts book naturally on right arm of King's chair, sitting sidewise.

189. "... he said I was a fishmonger..."

A look of disgust.

192. "What do you read, my lord?"

Polonius approaches Hamlet.

193. "Words, words, words."

Booth bends the book over so that Polonius can overlook it, answers and then resumes reading, turning over a leaf.

195. "Between who?"

Looking up from his book.

197. "Slanders, sir, for the satirical rogue..."

Tapping the book with his left hand.

198–202. "... that old men have... weak hams..."

Apparently reading aloud from the book.

205. "... old as I am..."

Spoken rather mournfully.

206. "... like a crab, you could go backward."

Imitating motion of a crab with fingers of right hand, [then] resuming his reading.

210. "Into my grave?..."[4]

In a tone of surprise at such a question and looking up from his book.

---

4. See Shattuck (165n.13) regarding Booth's speaking this line as a question rather than a declaration.

217. "My honorable lord..."

Booth rises impatiently as if he could no longer endure the stupid old man's interruptions.

218. "... take my leave of you."

Booth looks delighted and relieved.

219. "You cannot, sir..."

Booth half sarcastically, half politely to Polonius.

221. "... except my life..."

Spoken in an utterly changed, a lower, and an indescribably sad, weary, despairing tone, while he slowly walks towards left front corner and turns round towards his right hand, thus bringing his back to audience for his next speech [223] "These tedious old fools."

224. "You go to seek the Lord Hamlet."[5]

Walking towards center-back and looking out between the parted curtains into the lobby with his book still in his hand.

228. "My excellent good friends!"

Booth turning as they speak, sees and recognizes them. His face lights up with pleasure, even to a welcoming smile; he walks hastily over to them as he goes, closing his book and tossing it <u>so gracefully</u> on to table, following it with his eyes. He shakes hands with both of them warmly.

Again his natural manner with Rosencrantz and Guildenstern, directly after his <u>apparent</u> foolishness and <u>real</u> sarcasm and wit with Polonius, shows that he is quite sane.

279. "To visit you, my lord..."

---

5. In the *Prompt Book* edition, following 223, "as Polonius retires, he meets outside, Rosencrantz and Guildenstern," who, following "God save you, sir!" to Polonius, enter to greet Hamlet 226–27. Lines 224–25, however, were spoken within the lobby.

[1883] Rosencrantz crosses over towards right. All, however, are standing at left of Queen's chair.

280–81. "Beggar that I am, I am even poorer in thanks; but I thank you..."

This said with exquisite friendly manner and tone of sincere pleasure and gratitude.

283. "Were you not sent for?"

[1883] Booth stands facing audience and putting a hand on the shoulders of Rosencrantz and Guildenstern. He looks from one to the other, asking his questions in a free, frank, friendly way; at the same time there creeps into his tone and manner a slight coolness, a difference from his first welcoming and his "I thank you" and naturally enough as he begins to suspect they have not come of their own affectionate desire to see him.

288. "Why, any thing, but to the purpose."

[1883] Removing his hands from their shoulders.

293–99. "That you must teach ... sent for, or no?"

Spoken rapidly and with moderate earnestness, especially at [296–98]. A trifle contemptuous and a trifle impatient and as if wishing he knew what string he could pull to make them open and frank. It is not said as if he had much heartfelt faith in the efficacy of his conjuring. Plays with his dagger while speaking.

[1883] Gesticulating with forefinger of right hand extended at ["That you must teach me"].

301–2. "Nay, then, I have an eye of you."

[1883] Walking back away from them behind table; tone of suspicion.

[1884] Walking away from them towards footlights, so as to have them behind him.

304. "I will tell you why..."

Sitting down on the end of the table nearest them.

[1883] Walking around table towards right and standing close to King's chair.

[1884] Walking over and standing in front of King's chair.

307. "I have of late—"

[1884] Sitting on table, or rather perhaps leaning against it.

312. "... this most excellent canopy, the air, look you..."

Rising and walking over to the window opposite them, at right of stage, pushing aside the drapery curtains and looking out waving his hand up to the sky.

[1884] Rising walking <u>towards</u> right and turning back to audience.

313. "... this brave o'erhanging firmament..."

[1883] Walking towards window at right, pushing aside drapery curtain, looking out and waving his hand skyward. The courtiers advance towards window as if to "look" as he bids them.

[1884] Waving his right hand back and forth towards wide doorway opening on to verandah from which can be seen a fine landscape.

315. "... why, it appears no other thing..."

[1883] Turning away from window and letting his arm fall heavily to his side.

[1884] Turning around towards his right hand.

316–17. "What a piece of work is man!"

Turning back towards them and speaking with a noble, earnest eloquence, looking heavenwards.

[1883] As before. With what eloquent voice!!

332–34. "... we coted them ... offer you service."

Booth starts, shrugs his shoulders, while a sudden gleam of delight shoots over his face.

335–36. "He that plays the king shall be welcome."

Throwing up his hand, speaking most cheerily and smiling; seems forced.

343. "How chances it they travel?"[6]

Rosencrantz and Guildenstern walk about a little, but keep generally on left. Around their necks are chains on which are suspended jeweled lockets supposed to contain miniatures of the present King of Denmark. Booth takes hold of these at ["How chances it they travel?"] and looks at them one after the other, while he talks in a somewhat absent manner, evidently with his mind on thoughts suggested by the lockets and not on his own words or theirs wholly. At "It is not very strange" etc. [380] roughly letting the lockets fall back on their owner's breasts, and speaking rather contemptuously. Sometimes he does this to Rosencrantz only, while Guildenstern stands at right back.[7]

385. "... there is something in this ..."

Stepping toward right front.

387. "There are the players."

Standing at right back of stage.

388. "Gentlemen, you are welcome ..."

[To Rosencrantz and Guildenstern] who approach Booth from either side, he standing near the middle with his back to audience.

389. "Your hands, come then."

Shaking hands with them in middle of stage and speaking in a tone of sincere cordiality.

391–94. "... let me comply with ... entertainment than yours."

---

6.   Booth cut 346–47, 352–79, thus 380 followed 351.

7.   Compare to Shattuck, 169n.18.

From his manner, we catch a glimpse of what a noble host in his own home, what a courteous, hospitable, free hearted, gay entertainer, Hamlet must have been before his father's death.

[1883] Spoken by Booth with equal sincerity but with less affection and more politeness in his tone.

395–96. "... but my uncle-father and aunt-mother..."

Rosencrantz steps toward left and Booth follows him as he says this line; both looking expectant of the Players.

[1884] "Uncle-father" to Rosencrantz, "aunt-mother" to Guildenstern; both with great emphasis of scorn.

398. "I am but mad north-north-west..."

Booth turns toward Guildenstern, steps up to him, putting his right hand on Guildenstern's arm and his face close to his as if imparting confidentially a great secret; as if it were a "good joke" and in a tone of derision, giving a slight laugh of scorn; his words are audible to Rosencrantz also.

399. "... I know a hawk from a handsaw."

All pass around behind table to right corner back and stand looking towards left.

400. "Well be with you, gentlemen!"[8]

Booth's manner to Polonius is the assumed crazy manner, similar to that [before Rosencrantz and Guildenstern's entrance] only exaggerated and seemingly to make fun for Rosencrantz and Guildenstern. But it is quite evident to all except Polonius that Hamlet is perfectly sane, and very witty. Nevertheless, his manner to Polonius retains a form of politeness sufficiently so that he does not appear rude to him. Polonius at any rate cannot take it for rudeness, believing Hamlet is crazy. Booth seems to derive a slight temporary amusement from this sort of intercourse, if by amusement we mean whatever serves to lull the mental faculties and banish reflection. Yet all the time it is evident that his mind is burdened with far weightier matters, and that his real interest lies elsewhere—deep within his own

8. In the *Prompt Book* edition, Polonius delivered this line "within."

breast. It is also evident that Booth's assumption of this sort of crazy manner is not <u>for</u> his own amusement primarily and chiefly.

When with Rosencrantz and Guildenstern from the first, an evident effort is exerted by Hamlet to treat them courteously, to entertain them, to carry on a conversation with them, as they would expect him to do; this effort is required, partly because he is suspicious of them, partly because his state of mind makes any conversation upon ordinary matters most difficult.

Booth makes this <u>so clear</u>. As they afterwards tell the King and Queen in part "cut out," [III.<u>1.11–12</u>][9] he receives them "Most like a gentlemen," but with much forcing of his disposition.

[1884] Booth seems from the first less cordial than before, more merely polite; you see more plainly that Rosencrantz and Guildenstern were never his loved friends, as Horatio was and is, but mere associates, acquaintances.

401. "Hark you, Guildenstern . . ."

Pointing towards left. Thro' the doorway curtained at left, they apparently can see and be seen by Polonius, as he approaches thru a hall or another apartment, before he enters the room and appears on stage.

405. "I will prophesy . . ."

Booth sits down on arm of King's chair with his back to Polonius as he enters and Rosencrantz stands in front of Booth.

408. "My lord, I have news to tell you."

[Polonius] advancing across stage and in front of table about to middle.

409. "My lord, I have news to tell you."

Booth rises, walks quickly over to meet him, and takes him by the hand addressing him confidentially.

[1883] Said in mocking mimicry of Polonius.

411. "The actors are come hither . . ."

---

9. Booth cut these lines.

Booth glances over to Rosencrantz and Guildenstern and I think he winks at them; at any rate he looks roguish, as if he would say "There! did not I tell you so?!"

412. "Buz, buz!"

Booth drops Polonius's hand.

413. "Then came each actor on his ass,—"

In a sing-song tone.

415–21. "The best actors ... are the only men."

Booth appears to listen attentively, shrugs his shoulders, pinches his mouth, and assumes a comical look of much admiration. Stands facing audience.

[1883] Hamlet looks straight ahead towards audience and seems to be thinking of something else than what Polonius is saying—yet nothing especially sad or deep.

422–23. "O Jephthah, judge of Israel, what a treasure ..."

Folding his hands as in pictures do children in saying their prayers and looking upward. Booth's delivery of this exclamation is very complex. His voice is sweet and musical, his manner serious and almost reverential, his tones such as one would naturally use who had just read and been impressed by the Bible story (Judges XI).[10] At the same time his manner indicates that he intends it as an ironical reference to old Polonius's extravagant praise of the actors, these being his wonderful "treasure," as it were, which he brings to the Lord Hamlet to please him and divert his mind from melancholy musings. At the same time also, Booth infuses into his tone a certain dreamy earnestness of his own personality which makes you ask "Is he not thinking of Ophelia?"

424. "What treasure had he, my lord?"

As usual Polonius takes Hamlet literally and sees not at all the keen wit which is playing with him. To Polonius this answer seems utterly irrelevant

---

10. A reference to the source for the story of Jephthah and his daughter, Judges XI: 34–40.

and but another sign of Hamlet's craziness which is just what Hamlet intended him to conclude, as Booth indicates.

426–27. "One fair daughter, and no more…"

In a recitative style and a light, careless tone.

432. "Nay that follows not."

Apparently meaning "Nay, what you have just said is not what comes next—the next line—in the verse I am quoting."

435. "As by lot, God wot…"

Turning round so as to face Polonius, thereby fronting towards stage left; taking the old man's hand in his own left hand and pointing upward with his right hand.

436. "… and then, you know…"

Booth pretends and does delude Polonius into believing that he is really recalling some verses he has read, set down so and so by good authority; but he makes it evident that really he is composing the lines on the spur of the moment and perhaps a trifle "put to it" for rhymes, because he does not care to give much of his attention to it now. From [Polonius's entrance] to [the entrance of the Players,] his tone and manner is peculiarly sportive and innocent, almost childlike.

Following 439. Enter several Players L.

Booth drops the hand of Polonius and drops him and all his talk at the same time and advances to greet the Players with a resumption of his own natural manner, and speaks to them in a tone almost jocund in its hearty welcome; at the same time he expresses a shade of condescension of a patron—which is suitable.

442–43. "O, my old friend! thy face is valanced since I saw thee last…"

Addressing First Player and referring to his beard grown since he saw him act last.

443–44. "Comest thou to beard me in Denmark?"

Booth smiles.

450. "We'll e'en to't like French falconers..."

[1884] Booth rubs the palms of his hands together. Speaks in a bright, interested tone and manner.

456. "... but it was never acted; or if it was..."

Making his own peculiar gesture of a graceful little wave of the hand and wrist.

470. "... begin at this line..."

Gesture with pointed forefinger at First Player.

471. "... let me see, let me see—"

As if cogitating, glances up at the ceiling. Striding the floor. Remarkable is the art by which Booth makes so noticeable the difference between the earlier situation [at 435–36] when Hamlet is pretending to recall certain lines, and the situation here where Hamlet is really trying to remember.

472. "'The rugged Pyrrhus...'"

A little uncertainly.

473. "... it is not so:—it begins with Pyrrhus:—"

Putting his hand up to his head as everyone does when trying to recollect anything.

[1884] Smiling pleasantly at himself. Rosencrantz and Guildenstern are still on right of stage; and Polonius also, but nearer middle than to others so as to speak easily to Hamlet.

474–86. "'The rugged Pyrrhus, he whose sable arms...'"[11]

He has recalled the lines, at last, correctly. Throwing back his head and brandishing his right arm he delivers with good oratorical effect, but in a

---

11. Booth cut 476–85.

declamatory style. It is Hamlet <u>acting</u>, and very different from Hamlet <u>living</u> and <u>speaking</u>, as we have hitherto seen him. Yet in both cases it is Edwin Booth acting!!

488. "Fore God, my lord . . ."[12]

Polonius interrupts Booth in saying this.

[1884] Polonius applauds Hamlet by clapping.

487. "So proceed you."

Thus checked in mid career, for a second Booth appears angry at Polonius's officious patronizing interruption of approval; but immediately perceives the humor of the situation and perhaps also recollects that he must act toward Polonius in his assumed "crazy manner" as he "puts a double varnish on" the absurd patronage of Polonius by making him a low bow of much deference and gratitude while a slight satirical smile plays about the corners of his mouth. Addressed to the First Player. Another player places one of the old quaint armchairs near Hamlet which service he acknowledges by a slight gesture and Booth seats himself in an easy graceful attitude, leaning against one of its arms and facing First Player to whom he pays close attention.

521. "It shall to the barber's . . ."

Booth turns his face over his shoulder towards Polonius with a comical expression of derision which reminds me of J.R.'s "O Lord!"[13] and speaks in a tone of impudence which would be downright insulting if it were not spoken under cover of his "craziness."

[1884] Booth also playfully snatches at Polonius's beard and just lightly touches it.

524. "But who, O who had seen the mobled queen—'"[14]

Turning his face partly towards audience from its previous profile, and gazing at footlights.

---

12.   In the *Prompt Book* edition, Polonius's 488–89 preceded 487.

13.   The reference to "J. R." is obscure.

14.   After 1878, Booth substituted "inobled" for "mobled." See Shattuck, 174n.21.

526. "That's good; 'mobled queen' is good."

Booth is too absorbed to notice this comment.

[1884] Booth does notice this with a similar half smile as before and a nod, a look of pitying, amused contempt.

527. "'Run barefoot up and down...'"

With a sigh, Booth turns his attention again to the Player.

544. "'Tis well; I'll have thee speak out the rest soon."

In Booth's tone lurks the tang of his thought—"At some time and place where we shall not be bothered with this old fool." He himself evidently admires the speech and does <u>not</u> find it too long; and wishes the Players so to understand. By his own affable manner to Players and orders for their hospitable entertainment, he endeavors also to offset Polonius's rather rude treatment of them.

545. "Good my lord..."

With a gesture of his right hand turning to Polonius who approaches him.

552. "God's bodykins, man, much <u>better</u>..."

Rising and going close to Polonius and gesticulating with pointed forefinger. Spoken with Hamlet's own natural grace, without the irony of the "crazy manner."

572. "My good friends..."

Resuming his seat in arm chair at left end of stage, back of middle, putting right hand over his eyes with elbow resting on arm of chair.

Following 573. Exeunt Rosencrantz and Guildenstern.[15]

---

15. Booth rearranged these lines so that 572–74 follow 561. Thus Rosencrantz and Guildenstern are dismissed and do not hear the plans for "The Murder of Gonzago." See Shattuck, 181.

At right with obsequious bows.

563. "... can you play the Murder of Gonzago?"

Spoken eagerly [to the Player.]

565–68. "You could, for a need ... could you not?"

[1884] Dilating his eyes and speaking eagerly.

570. "Follow that lord..."

Meaning Polonius.

571. "... and look you mock him not."

With a slight and peculiar emphasis or inflection on "you" so as to mean "Because I chose to mock Polonius, do not you presume to do so," while the glimmer of a roguish smile can be discerned on his countenance.[16]

[1883] Same as above, only more emphatically "a point."

[1884] "... and look you mock him not" with a faint smile, but no reference as before to his own "mocking" of him.

575. "Now I am alone."

Spoken with a tone and manner of such relief; of one almost worn out with inward contending emotions and the effort required to converse with others meanwhile; and the necessity of locking all his real earnest thoughts and feelings hidden in his own heart.

[1883] Continues to stand and does not cover his eyes; not so expressive a tone, rather as if stating the fact.

[1884] Hamlet stands still for a long moment, looking down, then says ["Now I am alone"].

576. "O, what a rogue and peasant slave am I!"

---

16. Stone's perception of this reading supports Booth's intention as revealed in his notebook. See Shattuck, 176n.23.

[1884] Sitting down in low chair in front of table.

577. "Is it not monstrous that this player here..."

[1883] Sits Queen's chair.

585–88. "What's Hecuba to him ... That I have?"

[1883] Increased emphasis and swelling tone and turning his look to right.

588. "He would drown the stage with tears..."

Rising then throwing out his arms downward with a wide spreading gesture.

590. "Make mad the guilty..."

[1884] Rising.

593. "Yet I..."

Striding across stage to right.

595. "Like John-a-dreams..."

[1883] Standing at right corner front and looking towards left footlights.
[1884] Standing at right corner and looking towards left ditto.

596. "And can say nothing..."

[1883] Emphatic and showing an indication of the coming sarcasm [598–616].

597. "... and most dear life..."

[1883] Slight display in his face of emotions of love and sorrow for his father.

598. "Am I a coward?"

[1883] Starting towards left.

602. "As deep as to the lungs?"

602. "As deep as to the lungs?"

Standing in front of King's chair and facing towards left front corner.

603–8. "Ha! 'Swounds I should . . . With this slave's offal . . ."[17]

Passing back again across front of stage and then round behind tables.

[1883. At line 603] turning round and striding back to right corner.

606–8. "To make oppression bitter . . . With this slave's offal . . ."

[1883] Turning towards his right hand and striding over to center of stage behind center table.

607. "I should have fatted all the region kites . . ."

[1884] Standing towards left corner back near Queen's chair.

608. ". . . bloody, bawdy villain!"

[1883] Said with great emphasis and distinctness and fierce invective tone, gesticulating downward with clenched fist.

611. "Why, what an ass am I!"

Pulling King's chair impatiently round, and sitting down in it facing towards right.

[1883] Sitting down in chair behind table and towards right corner back and facing audience.

[1884] Sitting down in King's chair, but on the side of it furthest from footlights.

617. "About, my brain!"

Slapping his forehead two or three times, [then] a pause of concentrated thought, of planning.

---

17.   Booth changed "Ha! 'Swounds" to "Why."

617. "I have heard..."

You can see by the growing eagerness of apprehension in his face, the growth of ideas in his mind and how the device takes shape and color in his thoughts. Booth in this soliloquy by severe self-reproaches lashes himself into a constantly increasing rage and excitement, hurling upon his own back the bitterest sarcasm, especially at [602 and 611–16].

623. "I'll have these players..."

Rising and speaking in a tone of decision and satisfaction.

625. "I'll observe his looks..."

[1883] Walking forwards on right of table.

626. "... if he but blench..."

[1883] Still further forwards towards footlights.

627. "I know my course."

[1883] In a tone of complete determination without a shade of doubt, or dislike of the deed.

628. "May be the devil: and the devil hath power..."

Looking horrified and speaking in a tone subdued by a weird dread and terror of the possiblity; Booth now stands in front of table facing towards left front corner of stage.

632. "Abuses me to damn me..."

[1883] Giving his peculiar startled shrug of the shoulders, and another look of horror.

[1884] Covering his eyes with his hand

632. "I'll have grounds..."

Walking off towards left as if to leave the room.

633. "... the play's the thing..."

Pausing, speaking in a tone like that at [623] only of tenfold intensity with a ring of anticipated triumph in it, and swinging his right arm.

634. "Wherein I'll catch ..."

Turning quickly round and facing in opposite direction, stretching out his hands and clutching the air, [then] a theatrical pause.

634. "... the conscience of the king."

With force and distinctness.

Following 634. Exit Hamlet L.

Quickly and as if going straight to execute his purpose. Exit at entrance nearest footlights at left.

Great applause and a "recall" before the curtain.

[1883] Booth makes plainer than before that the idea of the mimic play to test the king is not just come to his mind; rather as if he checked his own impetuous self-upbraidings, and turning from emotions to practical planning, reconsidered and definitely arranged and amplified an idea that had before shot into his mind. Many of his inflections are wonderfully fine in this soliloquy.[18]

---

18. Compare Stone's notes on this soliloquy to Clarke's in Shattuck, 176–79.

Act III

Scene 1

The Same as Act Second. The King and Queen seated at table C., and Polonius, Ophelia, Rosencrantz, and Guildenstern, standing near are discovered.[1]

[Globe edition III.1. 196 lines cut to 185]

The time of this scene is the day after the previous scene as shown by Rosencrantz [referring to line 121. "This night to play before him"] and it is in daytime, probably forenoon, because after the interview with Ophelia, Hamlet must have time to recover himself before giving advice to players.

26. "Good gentlemen, give him a further edge..."

Rising and walking towards Rosencrantz and Guildenstern.

28. "Sweet Gertrude, leave us too..."

Turning and making back towards Queen.

37. "I shall obey you."

[King retires] into lobby stage right ⌐y entrance at center back. [Queen] rising and walking towards left front and turning round towards Ophelia, who has been standing behind Queen's chair in whispered conversation with her father.

---

1. See Shattuck, 182–85, for a description of the setting for this scene in the Booth's Theatre production. As Shattuck notes, however (182n.1), and as the *Prompt Book* edition also indicates, later productions do not call for a change of setting.

38. "And for your part, Ophelia, I do wish ..."

Ophelia advances toward Queen.

40. "... so shall I have your virtues..."

Queen extends her hand and Ophelia takes it.

43. "Madam, I wish it may."

Ophelia kisses hand of Queen.

56. "To be, or not to be..."[2]

In Booth's soliloquies there is none of the raving of insanity;—it is preposterous to suppose him crazy. It is marvellous, even miraculous with what freshness and force and originality Booth delivers this famous, but hackneyed soliloquy—or rather thinks it out loud. You can see the thoughts slowly rise as for the first time in his mind, so vividly are they painted on his speaking countenance, portrayed in his walk and attitudes; his whole bearing shows him utterly absorbed in deepest meditation and profound melancholy, so that he realizes not his own body, whether he sits or stands, sees or hears, but does all this mechanically. His very voice is lower and deeper than usual, sometimes sounding sort of muffled.

At first he is discovered in the door-way at left, holding on to the curtain, apparently leaning against it. There he stands some time, motionless and silent, brooding on thoughts too great for utterance. His dress conveys the impression of being somewhat disordered, though in what respect is not definable. Afterwards you perceive that he is dressed as in Act II, though at no time in his acting did it require such an effort for me to notice his dress, as in this soliloquy. The man's <u>soul</u> is what attracts your whole attention. He walks slowly into the room with eyes fastened upon floor and head bent. Like drops from the deep ocean of infinite thought—like an approaching culmination to some previous train of thought, and yet a link between a past of thought unknown to us and a future perhaps never to be fathomed by himself—"a sound between two silences." The words "To be or not to

---

2. Compare Stone's description of this famous soliloquy to Clarke's. See Shattuck, 186–89. "A sound between two silences" is possibly a paraphrase of "A sound so fine, there's nothing lives/'Twixt it and silence" (J. S. Knowles, *Virginius* [1820], V.2).

be—that is the question" fall from his lips unconsciously, slowly in a low voice. Then absently he sinks down upon one of those quaint chairs at left back of stage resting his right arm upon the arm of chair with hand hanging from its end.

64. "Devoutly to be wish'd."

Lifting his eyes to heaven.

65. "To sleep: perchance to dream . . ."

Then slowly like the flushing dawn there rises in his face and radiates from his dilating eyes the thought of what that future life may be,—and the wonder and the awe-fulness of it seem to draw him up on to his feet.

65. ". . . ay—there's the rub . . ."

Stepping quickly forward with uplifted finger. Booth stands still most of the times and uses less gesticulation than usual, which is suitable. The varying expressions of his face are everything; and these seem not voluntary contortions for a purpose, but like the alternating gray shadows and gleams of light, the hollows and the swelling billows, that sweep like emotions over the face of the ocean, as the sun and wind command.

70–74. "For who would bear . . . of the unworthy takes . . ."

Spoken rapidly.

75–76. "When he himself might . . . With a bare bodkin?"

Slowly draws the dagger from its sheath in his belt, but not at all as if he meant to stab himself. Then shoves it back in again and lets go of it.

78. "But that the dread of something after death . . ."

[For] a moment o'er his face was traced the tablet of unutterable thoughts.

79–80. "The undiscover'd country . . . puzzles the will . . ."

Spoken in a tone infused with the sweetly solemn mystery of thought.

How could Hamlet say this, when he had recently seen his father's Ghost, a returned traveller, surely from that unknown land? See Coleridge.[3]

83. "Thus conscience does make cowards of us all . . ."

Emphatic gestures with clenched fist, while walking rapidly towards right.

85. "Is sicklied o'er with the pale cast of thought . . ."

Turning and walking back towards left and near footlights.

88. "And lose the name of action—"

Said with the tones of calm philosophical reflection, somewhat tinged with impatience and disgust, perhaps as thinking how the words apply to his own vacillation. The manner does not indicate sadness particularly, but meditation in some of the most profound problems known to the human intellect, problems in which his whole mind is earnestly interested, concerning which, moreover, there is no friend of equal faculties with whom he can commune.

88. "Soft you now!"

Booth stands at left front with back to audience; he lifts his finger as if hushing some one—i.e., himself.[4]

89. "Nymph, in thy orisons . . ."

Turning towards his left hand, he approaches Ophelia who stands still in front of King's chair; his manner and voice exhaling tenderness and deference and welcome; the voice peculiarly melodious, and the prayer it utters most evidently sincere. He bows low and gracefully and, I fancy, meant to kiss her hand.[5]

---

3. Numerous Shakespearean commentators have attempted to justify, as H. H. Furness wrote, "the apparent oversight contained in the assertion that no traveller returns from that bourn, when Hamlet had himself seen and talked with such a traveller." Samuel Taylor Coleridge wrote on this point: "If it be necessary to remove the apparent contradiction,—if it be not rather a great beauty,—surely it were easy to say that no traveller returns to this world, as to his home or abiding place." See *A New Variorum Edition of Hamlet*, 213–14.

4. Clarke does not describe such a gesture. See Shattuck, 189.

5. Compare Stone's descriptions of the Hamlet-Ophelia interview with Clarke's reaction as recorded by Shattuck, 196–97. See notes 8, 10, 11, and 12 below also.

[1883] The soliloquy now is spoken with the same gestures and attitudes, and in the same beautiful voice and exquisite modulations, [although] "To be or not to be…" spoken in a whisper, inaudible, with the head thrown back and the right hand clasping the head in a conventional theatrical manner. But like so much of this 1883 performance, the rare intense spirit that was before [i.e., in 1881] infused into it, seems somehow lacking, though to me is the lack less noticeable here than elsewhere. Father is disappointed in this soliloquy; calls its delivery "approaching the commonplace more than he had supposed possible."[6] The details of his interview with Ophelia are so different that I cannot record them, at least not until I see him again. Far less satisfactory to me. He is more stern and cold, exhibits hardly more than once his love for her, and shows very little hidden distress of mind. Strange!!

Following 91. "How does your honor for this many a day?"

[Going] towards left. He seems taken back by her coldness, but then recollects that it resembles her recent withdrawal of herself from him.

92. "I humbly thank you; well, well, well."

His tone of sad calmness and assumed formal politeness is inexpressibly touching. He also remembers that he ought to give her up, that he has resolved to do so. Makes a slight inclination of body.

Between these "wells" there is a strikingly marked difference of tone and inflection. First "well" is spoken in a commonplace tone, as one would say "very well, I thank you"; it relates merely to his physical health. Second "well" expresses his perplexity at her cold and formal manner about which he perceives something different from her bearing towards him at any previous interview; as one should say "What does this mean?" Third "well" goes still deeper and is said still more to himself than the second; in a tone of resignation as if he thought "Well, whatever it may portend or end in, I must endure it."

93. "My lord, I have remembrances of yours…"

Slowly drawing from her pocket a packet of his letters to her tied with a red ribbon.

---

6. Obviously Stone was accompanied by her father at this performance.

94. "That I have longed long to re-deliver..."

Booth starts slightly with surprise which deepens into a shudder of emotion as he realizes what this means.

95. "I pray you, now receive them."

Transferring packet to her left hand and holding it out to him. He steps forward extending his hand to take the packet of notes.

Following 95. Hamlet here catches a glimpse of the King and Polonius, in their hiding place at back of the scene.[7]

Booth looks greatly surprised, starts violently, opens his mouth quickly, whirls round his back to her, while a look of suspicion, loathing, hatred of the evesdroppers, darkens his face.

95. "No, not I..."

His manner and tone towards Ophelia change to roughness and incoherency.

96. "I never gave you aught."

With a "devil may care" tone and manner, standing at left back.

97–101. "My honor'd lord... givers prove unkind."

Slowly advancing along in front of table, holding out packet to him, in a timid manner,with a world of regret in her voice. His face is almost concealed from her, but the audience can see his struggles to control his grief.

103. "Ha, ha! are you honest?"

Snatching the packet in such a way that the King and Polonius shall not see the action.[8]

---

7. See Shattuck (190n.11) on Booth's justification for this business. The Scott watercolor referred to above on page 47, note 3, shows the King and Polonius eavesdropping from the overhead gallery of the "Grand Hall of Audience" setting used in the 1870 Booth's Theatre production. Undoubtedly, the setting Stone observed was like the simpler "Hall of Arches" setting.

8. Hitherto, as Shattuck notes (191n.12), only one other witness, Edward Tuckerman Mason, recorded Booth's business with the packet here at 103 and subsequently at

111. "Ay, truly; for the power of beauty . . ."

Standing in front of her and speaking with vehemence.

115. ". . . but now the time gives it proof."

Throwing his hands out in front of him.

116. "I did love you once."

Retreating to his former station at left back and keeping his back square to the doorway at center. Unseen by anyone, he kisses the packet. Spoken in tones of earnest tenderness and pathos, that carry conviction of his love and truth to every hearer, even to Ophelia. See Mrs. Browning's poem "Loved Once"; 'tis all in Booth's voice.[9]

117. "Indeed, my lord, you made me believe so."

Booth thrusts the packet into pocket of his tunic, below his belt; and pulls thence a handkerchief, with which he furtively wipes his eyes; then replaces it so as to cover packet and choking down a sob, he speaks "You should not have believed me . . ." [118] in same rude, indifferent way. "I loved you not" [120] is actually flung at poor Ophelia, careless of the result. As Booth stands at left back, he is near the antique arm chair in which he sat during part of "To be" soliloquy. In his agitation he clutches hold of this chair several times, and absently hauls or hitches it near to Queen's chair.

121. "I was the more deceived."

Bursting into tears and casting herself down on to the low chair in front of table and dropping her face on table. Sometimes she sits in Queen's chair, and then Booth sits in soliloquy chair.[10]

116–17. Even Mason does not record, as Stone does, Booth's "kissing the packet" at 116. For a brief description of Mason's record of Booth's stage business see Shattuck, 110.

9. *Poems* (1844).

10. According to Shattuck (193n.16), Mason recorded that "in later exchanges [Ophelia] was not seated but standing throughout Hamlet's last two tirades." Both the James Taylor and Harvard 1890 prompt books (see Shattuck, 111–12) support this arrangement. Stone's notes clearly indicate, however, that, at least as late as 1881, Ophelia remained seated.

122. "Get thee to a nunnery: why wouldst thou be a ..."

Booth advances toward her, his face convulsed with poignant distress, his arms extended as if he <u>must</u> embrace her; then he checks himself. "Get thee to a nunnery" is said in a voice trembling with emotion and piercing from its tenderness, sympathy, and sense of relinquishment.

126. "I am very proud, revengeful ..."

Casting a fierce look towards the eavesdroppers in the lobby.

126–30. "I am very proud, revengeful ... act them in."

Spoken with reckless vehemence. She lifts up her face, wipes away the tears, and turns her head away from him.

130. "What should such fellows ..."

Rising.

131–32. "We are arrant knaves, all ..."

Walking away from Ophelia as if about to leave the room by doorway at left where he entered [for "To be, or not to be ..."].

132–33. "Go thy ways to a nunnery."

Booth goes back hastily to her and stoops down a little so as to bring his face close to hers; speaking in a voice audible to Polonius and King.

134. "At home, my lord."

Ophelia knows where her father is and what he is doing, but she does not know that Hamlet knows the same. Booth had at "Where's your father?" [133] suddenly wondered if Ophelia were as ignorant as he had been of the "espials," and it occurs to him to try whether she be privy to the plot and an abettor of it to <u>test her</u>. From her hesitating manner and downcast, tell-tale face, Booth is keen enough to feel sure she is lying; he has learned all and more than all he wished to learn; he knows that what she says is false and he knows that she knows it is false. His face indicates surprise, regret, almost disgust, and sorrow too. He would not have believed that she would thus willfully attempt to deceive him. His mind leaps at once to a conclusion which blames her for more duplicity than she deserves; perhaps he suspects that her past kind reception of his love and apparent reciprocation was but pretense. He starts a little away from her and looks down at her with the above feelings expressed in his face. Not looking at him, Ophelia does not perceive what he has discovered.

135. "Let the doors be shut upon him..."

Said with special reference to its being overheard by Polonius towards whom Booth glances.

Booth shows in a most touching manner, in spite of the constraint he puts upon himself, his deep love for Ophelia and the agony it costs him to give her up and how his very endeavor to restrain his emotions and to conceal from the spies his real feelings, makes him unnaturally stern and brusque towards Ophelia.

137. "Farewell."

Does Booth kiss her hand? No. Or say "Farewell" coldly? Yes.

138. "O, help him, you sweet heavens!"

Ophelia is now convinced that Hamlet is actually crazy and thus prays for his restoration.

139–40. "If thou dost marry, I'll give thee this plague for thy dowry..."

Booth walks slowly round behind table, around King's chair, then rushes up behind Ophelia and standing thus delivers over her head his threat, "If thou dost marry..."

142. "Get thee to a nunnery..."

Bending over her and speaking in a voice quivering with emotion with passionate love and grief, from an almost bursting heart wrung by the agony of a relinquishment cruel to her and cruel to himself.

142. "... go: farewell."

Stooping, almost kneeling on one knee, he embraces her, placing his left hand with <u>infinite tenderness</u> upon the side of her head, his right hand caressingly upon her left arm, and kisses her forehead; his own face is hidden, the back of his head being towards the audience with its fine shape and wavy black locks against her golden tresses.[11]

143. "Or if thou wilt needs marry, marry a fool…"

Backing rapidly away from her, going back behind King's chair and table again, holding his arms out towards her and shaking hands with the spread fingers pointing at her,[12] and resuming in a measure the fierce, rough tone used at "You should not have believed me"—and "We are arrant knaves, all." [118 and 131–32.]

145. "To a nunnery, go, and quickly too."

His agitation seems to be rapidly overwhelming him; he raises his hands, palms towards her in desperate appeal, and partly turns away his face; he cannot bear another moment to look at her and keep his purpose of relinquishing her and he must do this latter. Nor can he continue the assumed farce of simulated madness, of sternness and indifference. "To a nunnery, go" is spoken rapidly and his voice grows shrill with the acuteness of his anquish.

146. "Farewell."

Rushing away almost out of the room.

148–49. "I have heard of your paintings too, well enough…"

Suddenly striding hastily towards Ophelia and fairly hurling the words at her. Booth must have made a terrible and desperate effort in returning and addressing Ophelia thus, and this effort he makes evident by the very exaggeration of his harshness and violences of tone and manner towards her.

154–55. "I say, we will have no more marriages…"

Advancing close to her and snatching her hands up.

---

11. Clarke does not describe this business. See Shattuck, 194.

12. Stone might have observed at this point the "cuckold's horns" gesture Booth thought appropriate at the word "monsters" (144). Mason also recorded such a gesture. See Shattuck, 194n.17.

155–56. "... all but one, shall live..."

Pointing upwards, speaking with emphasis, and glancing over towards the lobby, meaning for the King to take special note of it.

157. "To a nunnery, go."

Spoken in a voice changed enough and threatening to break; he rushes out of the room with hand pressed over his eyes. His exit is made by a door near the footlights left, rather than the one of his entrance [at "To be or not to be ..."].

Scene 2

A Hall in the Castle. First Grooves.[13]

[Globe edition III.2.1–96. 96 lines cut to 88]

Enter Hamlet and First Player.

The two stand in center front of stage, Hamlet on left. They enter from left, First Player coming in first. Booth wears his short "house cloak," I think, as in II.1, the same that he wore in the interview with Ophelia.

1–2. "Speak the speech... tongue..."

[1883] They enter from right, the Player first. This is said as they walk in. This "advice to the Players" is spoken as perfectly as ever.

5. "Nor do not saw the air too much with your..."

Really "sawing the air" stiffly with his entire arm. Then for contrast giving his own peculiar, waving, graceful gesture of the hand and wrist. Both [i.e., Hamlet and First Player] are now standing still in center of stage.

Booth delivers these speeches [1–40] in an absolutely <u>perfect</u> manner and tone. Calm, quiet, easy, natural, like one who knows from meditation and

---

13. See Shattuck (198n.22) for a description of the setting for this scene. The *Prompt Book* edition also indicates that "During this scene, set the Dais with chairs R., Platform L. chair and stool C." for the "Mousetrap" scene of III.3.

observation the theory and practice of acting; moreover with a certain lightness of manner and as if his mind was so great that these ideas were but surface ripplings. Very courteously withal to the players. A tone indicating perfect intellectual apprehension, but devoid of emotion.[14]

40. "... they imitated humanity so abominably."

Smiling slightly.

50. "Go ,make you ready."

Spoken very softly.

Following 50. Exit Player.

At left.

57. "Horatio!"

Booth takes a step or two towards right, apparently catches sight of Horatio at a little distance, and makes a sign to him. Horatio enters from right of stage and approaches Hamlet in an affectionate manner.

[1884] A faint, but very sweet and affectionate smile floats over Hamlet's face.

59. "Horatio, thou art e'en..."

Putting his right hand on Horatio's left shoulder and facing him; speaking in a tone of sincerity and heartfeltness, as if stating a truth.

65–67. "No, let the candied... follow fawning."

This might be intended to hit Rosencrantz and Guildenstern?

67. "Dost thou hear?"

[1884] Booth here puts both hands on Horatio's shoulders and faces him.

---

14. Compare to Clarke's reaction in Shattuck, 201–2.

76. "Give me that man..."

Stepping a little away from Horatio towards left of stage, fronting the audience, speaking in an orotund, emphatic tone.

78. "... my heart of heart..."

Tapping his own breast.

79. "As I do thee."

Stepping back to Horatio, clasping his hand, putting his left hand on Horatio's right shoulder.

79. "Something too much of this.—"

Slightly separating from Horatio, dropping his hand, etc. An utter change of tone.

80. "There is a play to-night before the king..."

Another complete change of tone; now like one who confides to a friend matters of particular importance; a lower somewhat hurried tone, while he appears to get very close to Horatio, to press into him his ideas, so earnest is he, and excited too. Booth puts his right hand on Horatio's shoulder, while with his left forefinger he lays down his directions playing upon Horatio's folded arms.

Booth's tender and affectionate manner towards Horatio is most touching. It expresses to the full the meaning of the text. He respects Horatio and loves him dearly; it is very plain. He trusts him, confides in him, leans upon him—the one true friend and faithful heart that he can call his own; and he evidently knows that Horatio loves him dearly too. Hamlet has evidently told Horatio the truth of his vision of the Ghost which he concealed from him and Marcellus. I think of all Booth's acting in "Hamlet," what makes the most lingering impression, next to that of Hamlet's innate nobility of soul, is his friendship with Horatio. Booth makes it ideally beautiful and yet most comfortingly real. It is indeed most touching.[15]

---

15.   Stone underscored this sentence in red, apparently to indicate that it was even more so in 1884 than in 1881. See also the comment of Mason regarding "Hamlet's affectionate intimacy with Horatio" in Shattuck, 201n.35.

[1883] The change here is to increased repose, quietness of manner, less excitement. It is spoken like a mechanical repetition.

[1884] All right again!

95–96. "They are coming to the play; I must be idle:/Get you a place."[16]

Walking quickly across stage, arm-in-arm, Horatio next [to] audience; exeunt at left.

[1883] Noticeable pause after "be." The word "idle" strongly emphasized in a peculiarily meaningful tone, while he taps his forehead, meaning "I must appear crazy"!!!

Scene 3

A Room in the Palace.[17]

[Globe edition III.2.97–417. 321 lines cut to 243]

Hamlet and Horatio are first in the room, entering at left-front. As King and Queen enter at center back. Booth bows respectfully again, but "with a difference." He bows when Ophelia enters, his back to audience.[18] Guards stand at back of stage, in lobby, in a military row, with helmets and halberds, etc. Booth wears his "house cloak." The time of this Scene 3 is in early evening of the day after the one on which the Players arrived. It is also the day after the arrival of Rosencrantz and Guildenstern.

[1883] Booth wears the black "student's gown."

108. "What did you enact?"

Booth's manner to Polonius is similar to that [in the earlier scene with Rosencrantz and Guildenstern]; he is evidently "chaffing" him. Polonius

---

16. Booth transposed "Get you a place" with "I must be idle."

17. Hamlet and Horatio exited at 95–96 and the scene changed back to the same setting as II.2—i.e., A Room in the Palace. In later stagings, however, as Shattuck notes (202n.26), there was no change of scene. For more on the setting for this scene for the 1870 Booth's Theatre production, see Shattuck, 202–4, and plates X and XVIIa.

18. This sequence of entrances in Stone's record is at variance with Clarke who describes Hamlet and Horatio entering at center back after the King and Court. Morever, Horatio entered leading Ophelia by the hand (Shattuck, 204). The direction in the *Prompt Book* edition is "Guards, Lords, and Ladies discovered. Danish march. Enter King, Queen, Polonius, Horatio, Ophelia, Rosencrantz, Guildenstern and Hamlet."

stands just at right of stage near middle. Other courtiers are farther at right and on either side of throne.

Ophelia has seated herself at center back on one of those quaint, old short-lounges on which she sits sidewise so as to face mimic stage which is on left. Throne [i.e., dais] on which are seated King and Queen is on right. At left hand arm of Ophelia's chair is a foot-stool, on which Booth sits, leaning sidewise on said arm, his feet towards mimic stage. From this position, partially hidden by Ophelia and her chair, he can watch King and exchange glances with Horatio who stands at extreme left, near footlights and at end of mimic stage, where he too can watch King.[19]

111–12. "It was a brute of part of him to kill so capital a calf there."

Booth passes around Polonius and then [at ". . . to kill so capital a calf there"] walks diagonally across stage towards left front, stopping when a little past middle of stage.

112. "Be the players ready?"

Turning towards his left hand and addressing courtiers who stand by the dais.

133–34. ". . . how cheerfully my mother looks . . ."

Queen sits smiling and talking to King; both sit on the throne. Polonius at King's right hand.

137–38. "Nay then, let . . . suit of sables."

[1883] Spoken in the mocking satirical tone of the entire speech, and expressive of no <u>intention</u> to don such a suit, nor does he do so at all in Boston.

151. "We shall know by this fellow . . ."

With a slight gesture of his hand towards said "fellow." Booth does <u>not</u> have anything in his hands to play with like Fechter. Ophelia uses her fan.[20]

---

19. Compare to Shattuck, 205n.30.

20. Fechter carried a text of "The Murder of Gonzago" and at the climax of the play within the play tore out the pages and flung them about the stage. Numerous Hamlets from Wilks to Irving toyed with Ophelia's fan. See Arthur Colby Sprague, *Shakespeare and the Actor* (Cambridge: Harvard University Press, 1944), 158.

162. "Is this a prologue, or the posy of a ring?"

Addressed to Ophelia. Booth rises uneasily from the footstool, moves it a little farther front and then reclines upon the floor in same relative position to the others, resting his arm on footstool and making his hands prominent on front edge of the cricket,[21] either in their grace of repose, or while nervously working as he grows excited watching the King, or in his gesticulations.[22]

[1884] Booth lies upon a handsome white fur rug—the skin of some animal with long fur.

191. "Wormwood, wormwood."

Glancing sharply at his mother and grinding the words out between his teeth in a low guttural tone.

During the course of the mimic play, Booth and Ophelia make a dumb show of conversing; this Booth does most naturally. It is evident that they speak of trivial matters, criticize the actors maybe.[23]

226–33. "Nor earth . . . be wife!"

Booth listens attentively [to the Queen] with an expression of approval on his face.

234. "If she should break it now!"

Addressed to Ophelia.

239. "Madam, how like you this play?"

Reaching forward a little over his cricket, so as to bring his face beyond the line of Ophelia's chair, so that he can scan his mother's face. He leans non-chalantly on his left elbow with his hand under his chin.

---

21. I.e., the low wooden footstool. Although listed in most modern dictionaries, the word is rarely used today.

22. The McVicker's Theatre photograph of 1873 in Shattuck (plate X) shows Booth in a similar position. Clarke does not describe this business with the hands.

23. Clarke does not describe this business. See Shattuck, 206.

247–48. "The Mousetrap. Marry, how? Tropically."

Pursing his lips and considering. Booth said "Trope-y-cally," meaning figuratively, by the use of that rhetorical "figure of speech."

[1883] Turning his head so as to look at the King whenever he addresses him, [at e.g.,] "No, no, they do but jest, poison in jest..." [244–45].

253–54. "... let the galled jade wince; our withers are unwrung."

[1883] Here and [at "The Mousetrap"] Booth expressed not only the satire of the text, but the undercurrent of threatening exposure of the thing which is in Hamlet's mind. "No offence i' the world" [245] and [251–54] "but what o' that ... are unwrung" [are spoken] in a light mocking tone, with such a smile! The latter is spoken in keen satire, so far as one of "us"—viz., the King—is concerned.

255. "This is one Lucianus..."

Addressed to Ophelia.

258. "... if I could see the puppets dallying."

Putting his hand up to his mouth and speaking behind it off to one side in the usual way when one wishes to prevent some one near from overhearing.[24]

263. "Begin, murderer..."

Addressed to the Second Actor.

263–64. "... leave thy damnable faces..."

Same gesture as at [258]. He does not wish Ophelia to overhear him saying "damnable"?

264–65. "Come: 'the croaking raven doth bellow for revenge.'"

In a low, deep tone, directing his words at the King, but not so as to be noticed.

---

24. Clarke does not describe this gesture. See Shattuck, 207.

266–71. "Thoughts black ... usurp immediately."

Booth leans forward over his cricket and does indeed rivet his eyes to the King's face, as if to pierce into his very soul. The King looks uneasy, "changes countenance," shuffles in his seat, hangs his head, and looks the very picture of alarmed, conscience-stricken guilt. No one appears to notice this appearance of the King, except Horatio and Hamlet. As he watches and sees the confirmation of the Ghost's words and his own suspicions subsequently, Booth's eyes dilate and glare at the King. Once he exchanges confirmatory glances with Horatio; his hands work nervously and prominently on front of cricket.[25]

272. "He poisons him i' the garden ..."

He rises hastily and in an excited manner addresses the King, speaking with rapidity and violence and with an appearance of wild delight.

274–75. "... you shall see anon how the murderer gets the love of Gonzago's wife."

His voice rises almost to a scream and extending his right arm, he points a shaking finger at the King.

279–80. "Give o'er the play. / Give some light: away!"

In his excitement, Booth snatches up his cricket and throws it towards left corner back and it falls with legs upwards. In the confusion of the outrushing of the throng at center back, Ophelia's chair is shoved towards left corner back over the cricket. Booth whirls around and tosses his arms aloft.

282–83. "Why let the stricken ... ungalled play ..."

Walking rapidly downstage towards footlights.

284. "For some must watch, while some must sleep ..."

Returning up the stage towards center back, and waving his arms out from his sides as if to move the crowd more quickly out of the room. Horatio advances from his post towards Hamlet.

---

25. Clarke does not describe any of this business with the "cricket" here or below at 313. See Shattuck, 207–8.

Following 285. "So runs the world away."

With a flushed face and an expression of the wildest exultation, Booth rushes, almost leaps to Horatio and throws himself into his arms, putting his right arm over Horatio's left shoulder and burying his face in Horatio's bosom. Horatio puts his arms around him in a affectionate and sympathetic manner. This lasts but a moment, then Booth lifts up his head with the exultant mood still possessing him and seizes Horatio's hand and shakes it violently as if in hearty congratulations and keeps shaking it through [300. "Upon the talk of poisoning?"] whirling Horatio along with him to middle of stage and speaking in a tone of triumphant satisfaction and certainty. Horatio, passing around behind Booth, seems to support him almost overcome with the appalling conviction succeeding to his first triumphal flush. But in a moment or two, there comes over his face a fearful change! Is it but a sympton of the natural nervous reaction from his tremendous excitement to a state of gloomy depression? It seems to me rather the expression of a convulsion in his soul. There suddenly sweeps over his mind an awful wave of recollection. Everything had been forgotten in absorption in the one vital point of convicting the King. Now Booth remembers not only his dire bereavement on the death of his father and the "deep damnation of his taking off," but there swoops down upon his quivering consciousness the nature of his own doom, his duty, made obligatory now beyond excuse or argument. The Ghost's tale has been proved true; then he Hamlet must fulfill the behest required by it; must obey the solemn injunctions of the veritable spirit of his father—must become himself a murderer! And then must follow horrible revelations to distract a happy court and plunge into confusion a tranquil nation! No small pang is caused by the thought of his mother's distress and the probable publicity of her complicity in the King's crime. Moreover, a deeper tinge of awe and horror is given to Hamlet's recollection of the Ghost's visitation now that he is convinced of the truth of its announcements. Booth's face grows ghastly with the agony of such thoughts as these, His "Ah, ha!" [302] is part gasp and he seems choking with horror. Spontaneous applause from audience.[26]

302. "Ah, ha! Come, some music!"

Spoken faintly to Horatio in a tone of entreaty, while still but partially released from his supporting embrace.

---

26. Stone's description of this moment is in several details much more graphic than Clarke's record. See Shattuck, 208–9.

302. ". . . come, the recorders!"

Walking off slightly staggering towards center back, clasping his forehead with his right hand, and speaking in a tone by no means gay (as might be inferred from the words; neither as if he were crazy and merry) but like a man struggling bravely to calm down his agony; like one who feels he dare not let his thoughts dwell on such subjects, but must have something to divert his mind or he shall go mad! It is heart rending to hear him. Possibly Hamlet was very fond of music and fled to it for comfort and refuge, for solemn soothing, and not merely for diversion.

Following 306. Exit Horatio.[27]

Horatio goes to fetch the recorders.

309. "Sir, a whole history."

Turning round to meet them, Booth with an effort gulps down his agony and speaks in an unsteady voice with a sarcastic tone. His manner bristles with resistances to them and displeasure at their coming, though towards them he assumes a decent form of politeness.

311. "Ay, sir, what of him?"

In a fierce tone.

313. "With drink, sir?"

Sneeringly. Booth walks over to Ophelia's chair which he has a little trouble disentangling from the cricket, pulls it forward a little and sits down.[28]

[1883] There is no entanglement of chair. Booth sits down about in the middle of the stage with his back (!) to Rosencrantz and Guildenstern.

316–19. "Your wisdom . . . more choler."

In a tone of sarcasm with a tincture of threatening.

---

27. Horatio exited at this point, as Rosencrantz and Guildenstern entered. Booth cut 304–5.

28. Clarke does not describe this business with the cricket. See Shattuck, 210.

323. "I am tame, sir..."

In an ironical comical tone expressive of humble obedience.

[1883] Turning partly round towards them still seated.

326. "You are welcome."

Rising, approaching Guildenstern and turning to him, bowing formally, as if greeting him on his arrival.

327–30. "Nay, good my lord... end of my business."

Booth then walks away from them.

331. "Sir, I cannot."

Turning around and speaking with slight impatience.

334. "... my wit's diseased..."

Touching his forehead.

334. "... but, sir, such answer..."

Approaching the two who still stand at left front corner of stage.

340. "O, wonderful son..."

Lifting his hands in the usual manner to express surprise.

341–42. "But is there no sequel...?"

Folding his arms and looking steadily and watchfully at Rosencrantz and wearing an air of schooling himself to patience to endure their presence and speech.

345–46. "We shall obey, were she ten times our mother."

With exaggerated emphasis. There is a bitterness in his irony which differeniates it from the earlier employed with Polonius.

346. "Have you any further trade with us?"

Spoken haughtily and impatiently and having walked away from them a little space.

[1883] Tapping his own breast [at "us"].

349. "So I do still, by these pickers and stealers."

Going up in front of Rosencrantz at stage left and holding up in his face his crooked fingers.[29]

354. "Sir, I lack advancement."

Drawing himself up and folding his arms assuming the tone and manner of a disgruntled politician, or disappointed office seeker, and glancing at them over his left shoulder.

[1884] In a very quiet manner, <u>dry</u> tone, ironical, of course.

358–59. "Ay, sir, but 'While the grass grows,'—the proverb is something musty."

Turning and closely approaching Rosencrantz with pointed forefinger, [then] moving away from Rosencrantz and Guildenstern towards right.

360. "O, the recorders! let me see one."[30]

Addressed to Horatio.

361. "... why do you go...?"

Seating himself near the middle of stage, Guildenstern on right of stage, Booth addresses Guildenstern. Here he drops the "crazy manner" assumed at their entrance. Booth says that his "wit's diseased," but he has almost <u>none</u> of his former "crazy manner."

---

29. Compare this gesture to Clarke's description in Shattuck, 211.

30. In the *Prompt Book* edition the direction following this line is "Hamlet takes one of the flutes. Guildenstern passes to the R. of Hamlet, as if to overhear what may pass between him and Horatio." Following 361: "Exeunt Horatio and the musicians R."

366. "Will you play upon this pipe?"

Offering the flute to Guildenstern.

370. "I do beseech you."

Addressing Rosencrantz, offering flute. Booth is seated in middle of stage, Guildenstern on his right, Rosencrantz on his left standing and bowing obsequiously.

372. "'Tis as easy as lying..."

In a tone as if he wanted to add "in which you find no difficulty."

372–76. "... govern these ventages... are the stops."

Fingering "ventages" and "stops."

382. "... pluck out the heart of my mystery..."

Clutching his breast and "plucking it out."

385. "... little organ..."

Holding up the flute.

386. "'Sblood."[31]

Rising angrily to his feet.

388–89. "... though you can fret... play upon me."

Spoken with a firm determination and with dignity. Booth then walks down towards footlights. Rosencrantz crosses over to right and joins Guildenstern.

390. "God bless you, sir."

Advancing up stage towards Polonius; pausing and bowing to him with exaggerated deference as he says "God bless you, sir."

---

31. Booth changed to "'Sdeath."

[1883] As Booth goes toward Polonius, he raises his right hand with an exaggeration of the gesture of blessing Polonius.

393–94. "Do you see... ?"

Polonius and Hamlet standing on left appear to be looking out of a window at the sky. Booth rather behind Polonius points over the latter's shoulder at the cloud. The window is behind platform which served for the mimic stage. Booth's manner toward Polonius is similar to that in [II.1 with Rosencrantz and Guildenstern] only the suppressed distress of mind is more perceptible, requiring a greater effort to assume this manner; there is no shade of amusement in Booth's manner.

396–99. "Methinks it is ... like a whale."

In a tone of irony as if not the cloud, but the extent to which he could "gull" Polonius was what he was thinking about—on the surface, that is.

401. "They fool me..."

Walking down towards footlights, and speaking as if to himself, and as if half amused, half disgusted.

402. "I will come by and by."

Turning toward Polonius.

404. "By and by..."

Still therefore with his back to the audience.

Following 404. Exit Polonius.

At center back.

405. "Leave me, friends."

Turning toward his left hand and facing them; speaking in a haughty, imperative tone.

Following 405. Exeunt Rosencrantz and Guildenstern.

At right, bowing low. Booth wheels around so as to front audience, then turning his face a trifle towards right, he watches them departing with a keen glance and looks after them with narrow, scintillating eyes; and on his face a shrewd, contemptuous expression, coupled with a faint prolonged "Humph" all of which plainly indicates that since he welcomes them to Elsinore as his good friends, he has discovered the worthlessness of their pretended friendship for him, that he despises their fawning upon him, knows why they are the subservient fools of the King, distrusts them utterly, in short, and is determined to be ever on his guard with them. Booth's countenance also expresses a certain degree of triumph over them, inasmuch as he has this time prevented them from "pumping" him, as they wished to do—and then to run like tell-tale to the King (compare Booth in interview with Osric [in V.2]).

[1883] Booth also shakes a finger at them and nods his head up and down with a slight pursing of the lips, all of which is expressive of suspicion ripening into certainty. He shows more amusement [in general], less distress of mind; or perhaps appears more controlled.

405–14. "'Tis now the very witching time of night... but use none."

If there can be selected any point where Booth lapses from the lofty plane of his usual rendering, always so superbly adequate to the situation, it is in this soliloquy which I call "not-Nero-solilo-quy."[32]

[1884] Booth redeems himself and gives this soliloquy very well with undaunted force and spirit.

405. "... witching time of night."

Midnight? Hardly so late as that because so much occurs, such long interviews before morning.

Scene 4

A Room in the Castle. First Grooves.[33]

[Globe edition III.3. 98 lines cut to 77]

---

32. A reference to 411–12: "... let not/The soul of Nero enter this firm bosom."

33. See Shattuck, 218–19, for a description of the 1870 setting for this King's Prayer scene.

This scene is late in the evening, after the mimic play, because Rosencrantz tells Hamlet that his mother desires to speak with him in her closet ere he goes to bed.

Following 72. Enter Hamlet.

Booth enters at stage right[34] in his tunic, bare headed and cloakless on his way to his mother's closet. On discovering King, Booth <u>starts</u> and exclaims.

73. "Now might I do it pat..."[35]

Whispers.

74. "And now I'll do't."

Drawing his sword and advancing towards King as if to slay him with it.

74–75. "And now I'll do't... be scanned."

[1883] Spoken too rapidly and disconnectedly, without the necessary pauses for the thoughts to arise in his mind and find utterance.

75. "And so I am revenged."

Stopping suddenly and turning toward audience as if his own words—"And so he goes to heaven" [74]—had arrested his hand.

76–78. "A villain... To Heaven."

So he stands considering with his sword held in front of him, pointing downwards in both hands.

[1884] Pointing his sword heavenward.

79. "O, this is hire and salary..."

---

34. Stone notes that "Sometimes [Booth] enters at stage left and goes out stage right" at the ending of this soliloquy.

35. In the *Prompt Book* edition there is a note that this soliloquy is sometimes omitted. As Shattuck notes (223) it is cut from the Taylor and Harvard 1890 prompt books. Obviously Booth was still doing the speech as late as 1884.

Figure 6. Booth as Hamlet: "And now I'll do't" (III.3.74)
(*Courtesy of the Hampden-Booth Theatre Library at
The Players, New York City*)

With a slight and bitter laugh.

82. "And now his audit...?"

Looking heavenward.

87. "No!"

In a tone of decision after wavering in perplexity.

88. "Up, sword..."

Putting his sword back into scabbard.

93. "...kick at heaven..."

Tossing upward his clenched fist.

95. "As hell, whereto it goes."

He passes across stage walking softly past the open oratory where King kneels, so as not to disturb him or be himself revealed. [Then] flinging clenched fist down towards floor, and glaring at floor. These are the motives of a fiend, but Booth does not appear extremely fiendish in uttering them. What most impresses you in the whole soliloquy [73–96] is the pausing for consideration.

95. "My mother stays..."

Meaning his mother is waiting for him to come.

96. "This physic but prolongs thy sickly days."

At extreme left, he pauses, looks back, and with a threatening gesture towards King, shaking at him the pointing finger of his right hand. Booth disappears.

Scene 5

The Queen's Private Apartment in the Castle. Dim light. The Queen, seated, and Polonius, discovered.[36]

---

36. See Shattuck, 223–24, for a description of the 1870 setting for this scene.

[Globe edition III.4. 218 lines cut to 144]

5. *Hamlet (Within) "Mother, mother, mother!"*

[1884] Hear Booth say this for the first time.[37]

6. *"I'll warrant you . . ."*

Queen seated in King's armchair in middle of stage with her left arm resting on end of table. Polonius hides in an alcove on left. Curtains are drawn away from window at right through which moonlight streams and gilds face of Queen.

[1883] Queen sits at end of table towards left of stage—i.e., in Queen's chair—reading from a large book; candle and moonlight as before. Table, chairs, Booth's stool and all are on stage right.[38]

[1884] Table is on right of stage. Queen sits in King's chair facing left and is busily reading. Booth passes as below.

Following 7. Polonius conceals himself behind the arras. Enter Hamlet.

Hamlet enters by a curtained door at center back, passes around his mother to right saying "Now mother, etc."

[1883 and 1884] Before stepping over threshold, Booth stands gazing earnestly at mother (unseen by her) with the uplifted curtain of doorway in his left hand.[39]

8. *"Now, mother, what's the matter?"*

[1883] Spoken in a quiet melliferous tone, yet as if stating indisputable facts.

9. *"Hamlet thou hast thy father much offended."*

---

37. Apparently it was inaudible at other Booth performances.

38. Prompt books of later stagings indicate that a stool was placed in front of the table, the "cricket" perhaps from III.3. This stool was used at 137. Where the Queen sat seems to have varied from production to production. See Shattuck (224nn.42,43). In 1881 the Queen was Mrs. Charles Calvert, née Adelaide Helen Biddles (1837–1921), a leading supporting actress. She also played Emilia during this engagement.

39. Clarke does not describe this business. See Shattuck, 225.

Queen speaks to him in a haughty tone of reproachfulness.

10. "Mother, you have my father much offended."

His answers mock her and yet his tone and manner express serious earnestness, and he evidently speaks truth. He is standing so as to face his mother, not near, a little to one side of her, near front right corner of stage.

[1883] Booth does not emphasize "my father."

12. "Go, go, you question . . ."

Making a slight quick gesture with his right hand as it hangs by his side.

13. "Why, how now, Hamlet!"

Angrily.

14. "No, by the rood, not so!"

Booth takes a step towards his mother, raising his right hand as if taking an oath; his voice assumes a higher pitch and a singing cadence which impart a peculiar intensity and solemnity to the words.

15. "You are the queen . . ."

In an ordinary tone of stating a fact and bowing to her official station, or the royalty to which he owes allegiance.

15. ". . . your husband's brother's wife . . ."

Turning his face a little towards his right.

16. "And,—would it were not so!"

Hanging his head and shaking it slowly and sadly, speaking in a tone of regret, as well as parenthetically.

[1883] Is so spoken that I understand it to refer to "Your husband's brother's wife."

[1884] Same as [in 1883].

16. "... you are my mother."

Bowing to her <u>motherhood</u>, and this time a deeper, far more reverential bow, and speaking in the tone of mournful, respectful tenderness, which Booth reserves for his mother only, and chiefly expends on the word "mother" inferring into that one name a sense of the loving depth and power of that holy relationship, as it mutually affects the parent and the child—so that my heart swells to hear it.

17. "Nay, then, I'll set those to you that can speak."

In a threatening "out of patience" tone and moving towards left as if to summon some one near; Hamlet supposes the King.

19. "You go not..."

Stepping towards her and seizing her wrist.

21. "What wilt thou do...?"

Greatly alarmed.

24. "How now! a rat?"

Leaving his mother and rushing towards the cry [23 "What, ho! help!..."].

26. "Nay, I know not..."

Leaping up in a <u>frenzied</u> manner and whirling and flinging his sword across the room over his mother's head.

28. "Is it the king?"

Hissing out the words while bending his body eagerly towards the Queen.[40]

29. "A bloody deed! almost as bad, good mother..."

---

40. Stone evidently saw similarities between Booth's delivery of this line and his delivery as Iago of a comparable line. She noted: "Compare Booth's Iago to Emilia, 'Hast stol'n it from her?'" (*Othello* III.3.310).

Rushing to the Queen, putting his excited face, with its rolling eyes, close to hers, grasping her arm savagely, while the words come seething through his set teeth. Of course "mother" not as at [8,10, or 16].

29. "... marry with his brother."

Booth lifts from the table the lighted lamp[41] and walks towards the alcove where Polonius was hidden.

32. "Ay, lady, 'twas my word."

Turning around and looking at Queen and speaking in a <u>stern</u>, relentless tone; which with his rendering of "Lady," suggests that he sometimes feels <u>almost</u> as if he could disown his mother when he reflects on what she has done;—<u>almost</u>, but ah! he never can quite!

32. "I took thee for thy better..."

I.e., the King. Replacing light.

34–88. "... peace! sit you down... And reason panders will."

Resumes her former seat. Booth strides up and down and across the stage with such impetuosity that to write a record of his track is very difficult.[42]

35–38. "And let me... against sense."

Booth walks behind table, around King's chair and over to left corner front.

39. "What have I done...?"

Queen is seated in King's arm chair.

40. "Such an act..."

---

41. Shattuck indicates (224) that there were "two or three burning tapers" on the table rather than a "lamp."

42. Shattuck notes (228n.49) that, in prompt books after 1870, Booth apparently sat at 34 and did not rise until the business with the pictures at 54. Stone's record indicates that Booth did not sit in 1881, nor in 1884. She does imply, however, that he may have sat for these lines in 1883. See line 53 below.

Booth is standing with back to audience at left corner front of stage; he throws up his head as he begins to speak.

41–48. "That blurs... a rhapsody of words..."

Striding up and down stage at left end and finally around behind table to window where the full moon is beaming in.

48. "... heaven's face does glow..."

Booth looks out at it and the light falls on his handsome face. Then he draws the curtains and crosses the stage to left in front of the Queen.

51. "Ay me, what act?"

[1884] Booth is standing near front center facing audience. He wheels around towards his left hand to look at his mother in amazement at her question and he echoes her words "What act!"

53. "Look here, upon this picture, and on this..."[43]

Pointing to the portraits one after the other. Two full-length pictures of the late King, Hamlet's father, and of the present King, his uncle, adorn the walls of the room; his father on wall of stage left. The Queen wears a necklace and locket (similar to those worn by Rosencrantz and Guildenstern) containing a miniature of her present husband.

[1883] Booth is seated in Queen's chair. The full length portraits of the two Kings hang on the wall at either side of the doorway at center back. Hamlet's father towards right so that when Booth apostrophizes [55–62] his back to audience considerably; and at [60–61] where he does as before, his back is directly to audience, and therefore there is no sight of his face as before.

[1884] Hamlet's father's portrait hangs toward left as formerly, so that we see Booth's profile well as he kneels at "This was your husband." [63]

---

43. According to Shattuck (229n.50) Booth argued against the traditional practice of having both pictures hung on the walls and does not seem to have followed it in most of his performances. He usually used lockets with miniature portraits which both he and the Queen wore. Stone clearly indicates the presence of two portraits in the 1881, 1883, and 1884 presentations. Whether he also retained the locket business in 1883 and 1884 is not clear from Stone's notes. See also her note to line 58 below.

55. "See, what a grace..."

Walking up stage, standing in front of his father's picture at left.

58. "A station like the herald Mercury..."

"Station" means "act of standing," "attitude"; hence the propriety of having represented a full-length portrait for Booth to gaze upon, instead of miniature in a locket around his neck as he did in Boston in 1880.

60–61. "A combination and a form indeed..."

Gazing at his father's picture and speaking in a tone of fond admiration which trembles with emotion. His face showing profile beautifully.

62. "To give the world assurance of a man..."

[1883] "Man" pronounced as "mahn"!

63. "This was your husband."

Kneeling before his father's picture and bowing his head in reverence and grief.

63. "Look you now what follows..."

Rising and turning towards Queen and rushing up to her.

64. "Here is your husband..."

Snatching up the locket that hangs on his mother's bosom.

65. "Have you eyes?"

Jerking locket violently and breaking the chain so as to leave the locket in his own hand.

66. "Could you on this fair mountain..."

Pointing to portrait of father.

67. "And batten on this moor? Ha! have you eyes?"

Flinging locket to floor. [From "... have you eyes?" to 70. "And waits upon the judgement: and what judgement..."] there is a constant increase of impetuosity and excitement in Booth's tone and manner.

71. "Would step from this to this?"

Booth hurries from a point in front of his father's picture to where locket lies on floor, stops suddenly; after the word "to" makes a pause, then utters "this" in a tone the <u>concentrated</u> essence of <u>loathing</u>, and he stamps his heel upon locket, I think.[44]

88. "O Hamlet..."

Queen cries and sobs and is convicted.

90. "And there I see..."

Booth rushes back to his mother and kneels beside her, while passionately talking to her [96–102] as she is seated in King's arm chair. In their eagerness and excitement Booth and Queen talk at once which is most natural.

Following 102. Enter Ghost R.

Booth starts up with a gasp and sways back against the front side of the table with a ghastly look of terror and recognition.[45]

103. "Save me and hover..."

In a faint voice of prayer looking heavenward. (Compare "Angels and ministers of grace, etc." [I.4.39].)

104. "What would your gracious figure?"

In a tone of yearning, awe-stricken supplication.

---

44. Clarke does not describe this business. In 1870, Booth flung the locket into the Queen's lap. See Shattuck, 230.

45. Booth thus arranged to have the Queen's back to the Ghost so that Hamlet must speak to the Ghost over her head or shoulder. See, e.g., line 109 below. See also Shattuck, 232–33n.54.

105. "Alas! he's mad."

To Queen the Ghost is invisible. She rises, having her back towards Ghost, and extends her arms towards Hamlet pityingly.

109. "O, say!"

[1884] Stretching his hands out towards Ghost over his mother's head and keeping them so, tremulous and approaching each other as if to clasp during Ghost's following speech [110–15].

110–15. "Do not forget... Speak to her, Hamlet."

While gazing on Ghost with dilating eyes and parted lips such a piteous pale face! (Yet by no means a face of weak fright, nothing which excites in spectator any feeling of contempt for Hamlet; no, indeed, rather a feeling of sympathetic terror; he makes it <u>so real</u>!) He passes tremulous hands up and down his mother's arms and slowly clasps her hands in a sort of mechanical way, a dumb instinctive clinging to any human being near one at such a moment of supernatural terror.[46]

115. "How is it with you, lady?"

Said in an extremely absent, mechanical way as in dazed obedience to the Ghost's words; also in a faint voice, putting tremulous hands around his mother's shoulders as if to protect or soothe her.

[1884] Booth drops his trembling hands on her shoulders in a protecting way, yet automatically, too, so awestruck that he scarcely knows what he is doing.

116. "Alas, how is't with you?"

Queen approaches closer to Hamlet, if possible, clings to him, gazing with wild anxiety up into his face.

127. "Do not look upon me..."

Addressing the Ghost. In this interview with Ghost, Booth imparts to his tone and manner a difference from that in first interview [I.4]; a difference

---

46. Stone's description of Booth's business here and at line 115 below is much more vivid than Clarke's. See Shattuck, 232.

surely felt, but difficult to describe. He feels <u>great awe</u> and <u>dread</u>, but mingled with these is veneration, affection, and the merest approach to filial intercourse. Now he knows it to be the spirit of his loved and honored father; then he did not. Then there was a freshness in the terror; now Hamlet has grown familiar with it in his thoughts.

[1884] It seems to me very natural that the Queen does not sooner look around to where Hamlet is gazing and pointing. She does not do so until [132].

131. "Do you see nothing there?"

Pointing with his left hand to Ghost who stands front right corner of stage.

132. "Nothing at all; yet all that is I see."

Queen turns and looks all around the room but sees no one. Turning back to Hamlet as if anxious about him.

133. "Nor did you nothing hear?"

Notice the change from present tense [at 131] to past tense [at 133]. This Booth makes apparent in his voice. At [133] he for the first time removes his eyes from staring at Ghost and looks at his mother, speaking in a tone of bewildered incredulity, great curiosity of her reply, and growing alarm.

133. "No, nothing but ourselves."

Booth gives a sudden cry of fright and horror, throws up his arms, and casts himself down on to Queen's chair upon his right side with arms prone on the table and face dropped on them. His fright and horror are occasioned not by the Ghost, but by the sudden thought that he himself must be going mad, that he cannot trust his own eyes and ears.

Unseen by Hamlet, Ghost moves slowly across stage left.

Booth rises, gazes towards the spot where he had seen the Ghost, right hand corner of stage, and, of course, sees nothing there. Booth seems to look and look again, though without once turning away his eyes. Then an expression of relaxation comes across his face and figure; he turns toward his mother, who is standing in front of Queen's chair at his left hand as he turns [134].

From [131 through 133] but a short time elapses and the continuity of the dialogue is so preserved that [134] seems spoken in reply to Queen's [response 133], though much significant action by Booth has intervened.

134. "Why, look you there!"

Booth catches sight of Ghost at left front corner of stage, his face lights up strangely, he speaks in a low excited voice and points to it; his tone also has a shade of triumph in it as addressed to his mother, as if she must now see it and be convinced.

135. "My father in his habit as he lived!"

Waving aloft his right arm and screaming out the word "father' in excited certainty that it is he. (Not <u>at all</u> as if addressing Ghost.)

136. "Look, where he goes . . . !"

Pointing again and speaking each successive phrase with increasing rapidity and excitement.

Following 136. Exit Ghost. L.

As Ghost disappears, Booth sinks down on to Hamlet's chair, this time on his left side, and drops his face upon the table, as if overcome.[47]

137. "This is the very coinage of your brain . . ."

Queen has sat down in Queen's chair. Her voice indicates that she is recovering from her "extreme terror"—

139. "Ecstasy!"

Booth lifts his head, takes his hand and with his own left [feels his pulse][48] and is speaking very earnestly, but compared with [earlier dialogue] quite

---

47. Shattuck (234n.58) notes that in 1870 Booth fell prostrate at this moment, but that he later eliminated this business. Other eyewitnesses observed that Booth knelt before the Queen who fell upon a stool near the table. Stone is the only eyewitness who records this business with the table here and below at line 150.

48. Stone omits a completion of this phrase. This gesture, however, is described by Clarke. See Shattuck, 234.

slowly, with no anger but a tinge of appealing fondness which deepens as he continues, and is mingled with a tone of solemn adjuration.

[1884] Appears to feel his mother's pulse.[49]

147. "It will but skin and film the ulcerous place . . ."

Moving his right hand around on his breast.

149. "Confess yourself to heaven . . ."

Looking heavenward.

150. ". . . avoid what is to come . . ."

Bringing his face in his hands upon the table as his head droops downward with the dreadful thought; distress is written on his face.

156. "O Hamlet, thou has cleft my heart in twain."

[Queen] rising and starting as if to retire towards left and with the air of closing the interview.

157. "O, throw away the worser part of it . . ."[50]

Lifting his head suddenly with one of Booth's rare, <u>spiritual</u> expressions on his face, a look of thankfulness and the hope of joy to come commingled; the look and tone spring from depths within his soul where dwells that holy love for his mother which seeks only the highest good of the loved ones. 'Tis such a look, methinks, as might have shone upon King Arthur's face at his farewell to Guinevere, when he says "Leave me that, I charge thee, my last hope!"[51] Only Booth, as fitting in a son, <u>beseeches</u>; King Arthur, as the husband and King <u>commands</u>; both with equal love, and longing, and earnestness.

[1883] None of this [above].

170. "Once more, good night . . ."

---

49. Clarke does not describe this gesture. See Shattuck, 234.

50. Booth is still seated at the table at this point according to Stone.

51. See Alfred, Lord Tennyson's "Guinevere" in *Idylls of the King* (1859–85).

Queen stretches out her hand as an affectionate adieu to Hamlet, who kisses it.

171. "And when you are desirous to be bless'd..."[52]

Pointing heavenwards.

172. "I'll blessing beg of you."

Bowing his head indicative of how he would ask her blessing—slight and brief, however, not as if he were actually begging it then.

173–78. "I do repent; but... only to be kind..."

[1883] Very little regret in tone.

177. "So again, good night."

Embracing her affectionately. Putting his left hand about her head with an exquisite tenderness, peculiar to this gesture of Booth's, and his right arm about her waist, he kisses her forehead, and addresses her, "So again, good night."

178. "I must be cruel, only to be kind..."

Withdrawing a very little from her and turning his face towards audience, pressing his right hand upon his eyes as if to keep back the tears, he speaks in a voice tremulous with emotion and as if to himself. [Then] again turning his face to her, he folds her in his arms with unutterable love and pity; she drops her head upon his left shoulder hiding her face.

179. "Thus bad begins, and worse remains behind."[53]

Looking upward and fronting audience. Drooping his head over her. Spoken as if to Heaven and his own soul.

Booth is wonderful in this interview. He reproaches his mother sternly, sharply, searchingly, even angrily, in hot, rapid, impassioned words. Yet his earnestness, his ardent love for his dead father, his respect, and even affec-

---

52. Booth omitted the "and" in the line. See Shattuck, 235n.60.
53. Booth ended the act with this line.

tion for his mother, while abhorring her deed, are all evident; he seems to be administering a deserved reprimand from the heights of his righteous indignation, and the facts justify his doing so; while his manner keeps the words from the least taint of impudence. In latter part, he seems to appeal to her overgrown better nature, believing still in its existence. And at the very last, the <u>tenderness</u> of his "goodnights" tone, gestures, attitudes are indescribably touching! An exquisite contrast to the stormy parts of the interview and an illustration of Booth's <u>marvellous</u> versatility and superiority. <u>Finale.</u>

Great applause and curtain is raised again.

[1883] Spoken louder and fiercer than before, yet with solemnity. An instance of the <u>mystery</u> of Hamlet being lessened by Booth. Much less tenderness with his mother, less <u>depth. More</u> like the anger and distress of any youth, fond of his father, at his mother's second marriage.

Act IV

Scene 1

A Room in the Castle.

[Globe edition IV.3.2–70][1]

Enter King.

From right.

Following 7. Enter Rosencrantz.

From left.

16. "Bring him before us."

King sits down at extreme right.

15. "Ho! Guildenstern! bring in my lord."

Waving his hand and shouting towards left.

Following 16. Enter Hamlet, guarded, and Guildenstern

Guildenstern enters first, then Hamlet walking hastily and freely, untouched by the two soldiers accompanying him, who are dressed in mail armor of glittering steel as at opening of play; they carry long halberds towering

---

1. Booth cut Act IV heavily, including all of scenes 1, 4, and 6. He retained only portions of scenes 3, 5, and 7—330 lines out of a total of 662. See Shattuck (240, 248, and 249) for a summation of these cuts. For a description of the setting used for this scene in both 1870 and later stagings, see Shattuck, 240n.2.

above their heads. Hamlet's dress is the tunic and "small clothes," but no cloak, no sword. Booth walks quickly to the middle of the stage; when catching sight of King, he stops suddenly, and bows with cold politeness—a mere form.

[1883] Booth does not bow to King; and at "At supper" [17 below] he has back to audience as he walks back center of stage and turns around to face audience and King who sits on his right hand.

[1884] Booth stops short and bows as of old.

16–17. "Now, Hamlet, where's Polonius?/At supper."

In a tone of authoritative demand, but calmly. Booth folds his arms and stands some seconds looking fixedly at King—a fine contrast between the noble and the base. Then he says "At supper" in a calm, measured manner, very distinct articulation, and in a tone of veiled sarcasm.

Booth wears a quiet, easy, indifferent air; looks roguish, if he can be said to look so, whose face expresses not a particle of mirth. As in some previous scenes, he seems fully to appreciate the stupidity of his companions, the tangle of the situation in which they are, their misunderstandings and to allow his wit to play over the matter like heat lightning; while at the same time his mind is so full of other and solemn thoughts, and so weighed down by these, that he has no <u>enjoyment</u> of his own wit, and seldom, if ever, <u>looks</u> gay.

19. "At supper! where?"

With surprised curiosity for Hamlet's meaning.

20. "Not where he <u>eats</u>..."

So far Hamlet's answers refer to the corpse of Polonius.

35. "Where is Polonius?"

Rising angrily as who should say "No more of this trifling."

36. "In Heaven; send thither to see..."

In this answer he refers to the spirit of Polonius—which Booth believes to be the only real Polonius, certainly now. Before answering the King's [question], Booth makes a curious gesture: a reply in pantomine to the angry authoritativeness of King's demands. Unfolding his arms, Booth gently waves his two hands outward, slightly bows his head, and covers his eyelids, and seems to me, as if he would say "I care not for your approval or disapproval. 'Tis not worth your while to be so angry; I shall answer as I choose and when I choose." Booth says "In Heaven" seriously—i.e., without the sarcastic tone at [20–22] or at [18.] But the sarcastic tone again is perceptible in "Send thither to see," though differing slightly.

37. "... if your messenger find him not there..."

At the word "there," Booth looks upward.

38. "... see him i'the other place yourself."

Pointing downward and using a concentrated tone of indescribable sharp contempt and very emphatically approaching King.

In this interview, all the true dignity of royalty sits upon Hamlet; King appears ignoble enough. Booth's acting is absolutely <u>perfect</u>: clear cut, brilliant, strong, <u>frosty</u>, like a diamond! A complete picture with the focus of light at ["see him i'the other place..."]. At the word "there," [37] Booth points upward; then at "See him i'the other place yourself," Booth steps towards King, running his neck out towards him, making a pointed, contemptuous gesture with his right hand, and using a tone of concentrated sharp contempt and hate, also with emphasis. This always evokes spontaneous laughter and applause.

[1884] Quite a pause after "place."

38. "But indeed, if you..."

Addressing the company generally and with studied carelessness as to Polonius. Like a veil over him is thrown the "crazy manner," so that his companions think him answering as straightforwardly as he can.

41. "'He will stay till you come."

There is a change in the sarcasm; it is directed more at Polonius, at the thought of his powerlessness to do otherwise than stay—i.e., the corpse— which is what they want to find. The tone resembles that used by Booth in the Grave Digger scene in talking to Yorick's skull. At the same time there is a touch of ridicule for Guildenstern.

49. "For England!"

Booth gives a slight start and shrug of his shoulders, raises his eyebrows, looks suspicious of some evil design on the part of the King. But immediately remembering that he must not betray his suspicions, he so instantaneously suppresses all manifestations of them, and in fact has reduced the above indications to such quick, delicate points, that they are barely discernable.

49. "Ay, Hamlet. Good."

Booth watches King very closely with scintillating eyes and speaks "Good" before King has finished [his line].

50. "So, is it..."

King advances towards Booth and tries to speak graciously.

50. "I see a cherub..."

Walking close up to King and looking curiously into his eye until he sees reflected in it the image of himself, who is the "cherub" he means.[2]

50–51. "But come; for England!"

Starting off towards left and waving his hand and making a complete change of tone to sort of gay abandon.

51. "Farewell, dear mother."

Turning back and making an obeisance to the King.

53. "My mother..."

In a tone of correction.

55. "... and so, my mother."

Again bowing low to King and speaking as at [51] in the peculiar, low, mellow tone of mournful respect in which he usually addresses his mother. Also putting his hand to his lips and waving it downwards as he bows.

---

2.   See Shattuck (242n.5) for Booth's explanation for this piece of business.

55. "Come, for England!"

Booth walks rapidly off towards left heedless of his "keepers" who follow. He waves his right arm and speaks "For England" in a loud, swinging voice, as if he were elated at the prospect of going thither. This is the last time the "crazy manner" is assumed.

57. "I'll have him hence tonight..."

It is now long after midnight and Hamlet's ship sails about sunrise of the day after Polonius is slain; King told Gertrude that night "The sun no sooner shall the mountains touch,/But we will ship him hence..." in IV.1. [29–30] which is "cut out."

Scene 2

A Room in the Castle.[3]

[Globe edition IV.5 and 7]

Following 20. Enter Marcellus with Ophelia C.[4]

Ophelia is dressed in a pure white gown of "nun's veiling" with long flowing sleeves of immense size; her hair is strewn at full-length and greatly disordered; of course she looks wild.

42. "Well, God 'ild you!"

Queen seats herself in armchair with footstool. At stage left is a table endwise to the audience and in front of it is an armchair with a footstool. Behind table and close against left is an armchair. At right are two arm chairs.

68. "I hope all will be well."

Seated on floor at right leaning against one of armchairs.

---

3. Although in his 1870 Booth's Theatre production, Booth played Act IV in a single set, later prompt books call for two sets with the scene changing following IV.3.67. See Shattuck (244n.7) regarding setting for this scene.

4. The Globe edition reads "Re-enter Horatio, with Ophelia." Booth followed the Globe direction in 1870, but in all stagings after 1878, Marcellus accompanied Ophelia.

71. "My brother shall know of it . . . "

Rising and speaking in a tone as if <u>then</u> surely something would be done about it; rather a threatening tone.

71. ". . . and so I thank you . . . "

Making a graceful bow at entrance center back.

72. "Come, my coach!"

Waving her hands as if to a servant outside.

73. "Good night, ladies . . . "

Bowing and kissing her hand to the right and left.

Following 73. ". . . sweet ladies . . ."

Speaking another "My coach, my coach."

74. ". . . good night."

Courteously and then tripping away.

Considerable applause.

[1883] Ophelia did nothing at all, but recited her verse.[5]

78. "When sorrows come . . ."

Standing at center back, and just turning back from watching Marcellus out.[6]

Following 108. Exit Marcellus. Noise within. Enter Laertes, armed.

---

5. Compare Modjeska's business in Shattuck, 244–45. The Ophelia in 1883 was Affie Weaver (1855–1940). The critic of the *Boston Daily Globe* (20 November 1883) commented that she "failed to satisfy the requirements of the part, and in the famous mad scene she was altogether below the proper standard."

6. Marcellus exited following the King's line (75), "Follow her close; give her good watch, I pray you." He re-entered at "What's the matter?" (98).

With upraised sword. Laertes is dressed in mourning which is, however, much trimmed with glittering jet.

116. "Calmly, good Laertes."

The Queen rushes towards Laertes, between him and King, and thrusting her hands upon his breast strives to prevent his threatened attack upon the King.

120. "What is the cause, Laertes ... ?"

King stands on stage left and in front of table which is set endwise towards audience.

126. "Let him go, Gertrude."

She obeys him.

128. "But not by him."

[Queen] pointing to King as if again to interpose her person between the two and thus protect her dear lord and husband.

145. "To his good friends thus wide I'll ope my arms;"

Opening his arms.

153. "How now! what noise in that?"[7]

Ophelia is dressed as before, a long garland of flowers trims her dress from neck downwards, in her left hand sleeve she carries many more loose flowers.

158. "Dear maid, kind sister ..."

Approaching Ophelia as if to accost and embrace her; but she does not recognize him at all.

159. "O heaven, is't possible ... ?"

---

7. The *Prompt Book* edition direction is "Queen sits L. Re-enter Ophelia." Compare the following description of Pateman's business as Ophelia to Modjeska's business in Shattuck, 246–47.

Turning away from her and looking heavenward.

175. "There's rosemary ..."

Giving the same to Laertes.

180. "There's fennel for you ..."

Giving to King who is seated at the end of table nearest footlights. Sometimes King stands.

181. "... there's rue for you ..."

Giving to Queen who is seated at front of table.

184. "There's a daisy."

Sitting down on the floor and emptying the flowers out of her sleeve.

190. "And will he not come again?"

Strewing flowers as if on the bier of her dead father.

Following 200. "And of all Christian souls, I pray God. God be wi' ye."

Approaches Laertes and peers into his face, appearing almost to be about to recognize him; then suddenly gives a piercing, blood-curdling, maniacal shriek. Then she goes out backwards, very slowly, sobbing and holding on to her head—an utter lunatic.

[1883] Gives a sudden wild look at King, a look of terror, runs forward to her imaginary bier, snatches up from it the strewn flowers, gathering them up in her skirt, and retreats supported by Queen, and staring in fear at King.

201. "Do you see this, O God? "[8]

Laertes falls into one of those quaint old arm chairs at right and drops his face down on his arm on the arm of chair overcome with grief.

---

8. Booth changed "God" to "Heaven."

202. "Laertes, I must commune with your grief..."[9]

King crosses over and stands behind him.

[Following IV.7.36 of the Globe edition]

Enter Bernardo.

At left and kneels to King.

36. "Letters, my lord, from Hamlet..."

King starts.

Following 163. Enter Queen.

Queen at center back.

165. "... your sister's drown'd, Laertes."

King drops down into chair in front of table and is quite affected.

Following 176. "Fell in the weeping brook."

The drowned and dead Ophelia is borne in upon a litter, her garlands hanging about her, her face slightly disfigured. The drapery around Ophelia, if not her gown, ought to be wet as if taken from the water.

185. "... I forbid my tears..."

Laertes approaches corpse, kisses her face, then at "Adieu, my lord" [190] addresses King in passionate tone. Then at "But that this folly douts it," [192] his voice trembles and falters with emotion and again he bows down over corpse weeping.[10]

---

9. Booth cut 219 and all of IV.6 and then combined the King's speech (217–18) with three lines from IV.7—4–5 and 36—and the entrance of Bernardo as the messenger. See Shattuck, 247, for a description of Booth's texual changes.

10. Booth ended the Act with this line. According to Shattuck (248n.16), Booth introduced this original business of bringing in Ophelia's body probably in the late 1870s.

Act V

Scene 1

A Churchyard. Two Grave Diggers, with spades, etc. Discovered.

[Globe edition V.1. 322 lines cut to 286]

Churchyard at night with a cloudy sky and occasional gleam of moonlight arranged to fall artistically upon Booth's face. Monuments are seen. One large flat gravestone at right front corner makes a convenient seat for Second Grave Digger and afterwards for Hamlet. Stage is very dim.

Sometimes this scene is represented as taking place during brillant sunset, which slowly fades to grey twilight. The time is the evening of the day after the day on which King receives letter from Hamlet.[1]

1. "Is she to be buried . . . ?"

Standing in partially dug grave.

3. "I tell thee . . ."

Sitting on said gravestone.

9. "It must be se offendo . . ."

Clambering up out of the graves.[2]

---

1. See Shattuck, 250–52, for a description of the 1870 scenic arrangements for this scene.

2. Compare Stone's description of the Gravediggers' actions with Clarke's in Shattuck, 252–53.

15. "Nay, but hear you . . ."

Rising.

16–17. "Here lies the water, good . . ."

Laying his spade down near footlights at right.

17. ". . . here stands the man; good . . ."

Setting up his pick axe at some distance from spade towards left.

17–18. ". . . if the man go to this water . . ."

Pointing so as to "suit the action to the word."

33–34. "Come, my spade. "

Second Grave Digger hands it to him and latter makes as if he would resume his work. The old First Grave Digger is evidently very much plumed up with self-conceit at his own superior intelligence, wit, and acquired knowledge and shows it in his patronizing airs to Second Grave Digger and his face of scorn at his stupidity.

51. "I like thy wit well . . ."

Laughing freely.

56. "T'ot again, come."

Giving him a poke in the ribs.

57–58. "Who builds stronger . . . ?'"

Slowly and meditatively.

59. "Ay, tell me that, and unyoke."

Leaning on his spade and looking very wise and superior.

60. "Marry, now I can tell."

Eagerly and hopefully.

62. "Mass, I cannot tell."

Stupidly and despairingly.

67. "Go, get thee to ... a stoup of liquor."

Preparing to descend into grave, spitting on his hands, rolling up sleeves.

Following 68. Exit Second Grave Digger.

At left carrying a small brown jug.

Following 72. Enter Hamlet and Horatio.

From left and walking along slowly at back of stage, Booth being next to audience and leaning on Horatio's arm. Booth has on fur cloak with the hood up and looks indescribably handsome, with an air of unutterable sadness shown in face, gesture, and above all in his clear, sweet, penetrating voice. As usual, you feel as if Hamlet and Horatio had been having, or were in the midst of, a long confidential talk befitting intimate friends; Booth makes perceptible Hamlet's affectionate feeling towards Horatio and his sole comfort in his friendship in an indefinable way. Booth looks throughout this scene divinely young and most divinely fair! You feel that Melancholy hath marked him for her own. He is like a man of sorrows, acquainted with grief. Though never during the play jovial or boisterous, yet in this scene, there is a marked change in his manner. Passion is stilled into an abiding sadness. The appearance of anguish of soul is intensified, and this is done not by an increase of demonstrativeness, but by an increase of restrainedness. Your memory retraces the trials through which his sensitive spirit has already past. He appears languid and tired, and looks worn by long vigils of thought and battlings with his fate. He looks very pale and wan, but the firmness and ease of his bearing prevent the slightest apprehension of physical failure. He is not "sick"—a spectacle always more or less disagreeable. Though he takes Horatio's arm, throws himself into Horatio's arms, etc., it is not from actual bodily need of support, but an indication of spiritual closeness, because his heart leans upon Horatio. His motions are all very slow. The music and the pathos of his voice thrill your very heart-strings. I cannot even smile at the funny appearance and words of the Grave Digger, not because 'tis in a grave-yard, nor because of Ophelia's untimely fate, but from sympathy with Hamlet. Sounding in my ears and making my heart swell, I seem to hear the deep and solemn organ-roll and a lone voice singing:

"Abide with me!
Fast falls the even-tide;
The darkness deepens
Lord with me abide!"

[1883] Booth does not seem so indescribably sad as before, nor so pale; there is no such thrilling deepening of the pathos of the situation. [With] his questions of the Grave Digger, there is not the former quickening to real curiosity and interest at [165. "... why was he sent to England?" and 173. "How strangely?"], nor the increase of weariness and preoccupation at [185. "Why he more than another?"]. But all the conversation with the Grave Digger has the tired, indifferent manner and tone described in earlier notes. He glances oftener to Horatio with a half-smile. On the whole he appears to derive more personal amusement and to be less absorbed in other thoughts.

69–72. "In youth when... nothing meet."

As [the Grave Digger] sings, he digs so hard, and his spade so hits against tough obstacles, that his voice is shaken and even stopped; he quavers and grunts and goes on singing.

77. "'Tis e'en so..."

Standing still near his place of entrance, side to audience, but face turned a little more towards front as he gazes at Grave Digger. He nods slowly in assent to Horatio's words and makes a slight gesture with the right hand whose arm is leaning on Horatio's. Then stands silent for some time.

79–84. "But age with his... could sing once..."

[During Grave Diggers song, 79–82,] both [Hamlet and Horatio] walk more rapidly in a straight line across stage, stopping at middle, turning so as to front footlights, still arm in arm, and stand watching Grave Digger. Then Booth says [83] "That skull had a tongue in it, etc."

89. "It might, my lord."

They walk towards right front around grave stone on side of it towards stage right.

100–101. "... mine ache to think on't."

They stand sidewise, Horatio next to audience, and Booth a trifle in advance of him, his profile being impressive.

106. "There's another ..."

At right front corner.

127. "Whose grave's this, sirrah?"

Withdrawing his arm from Horatio's and advancing towards Grave Digger. The question is asked more to serve as a remark, than as if he really desired to know whose grave, or supposed it imported anything to him. Even more markedly then the page, this talk comes from the surface of his mind. Same tone and manner for most of the questions.

141. "What man dost thou dig it for?"

Booth sits down on flat gravestone at right with marvellous grace and repose of manner. Horatio stands at Booth's right hand and a little behind him, so the latter is entirely visble to audience. Booth's manner to Grave Digger is an indication of his naturally affable disposition—as Hamlet, i.e.

[1883] Booth sits on the base of a monument which rises above his head and somewhat interferes with the free turning of his head to glance at Horatio—which he does oftener than before. This monument is nearer center and is not the one on which he afterwards sinks down [—i.e., at the entrance of the funeral cortege].

148. "How absolute the knave is!"

Turning his head slowly and looking up at Horatio with a keen appreciation of the situation while a fleeting smile gleams for a moment over the settled sadness of his face. And the moonlight falls upon his face.

165. "Ah, marry, why was he sent into England?"

For the first time roused to a direct and special interest in the conversation, he glances at Horatio as if thinking "Here's an opportunity of hearing what the common people thought of my being sent away, and if there's any suspicion abroad at the King's real intention." He asks the question in an emphatic tone of curiosity weighted with unspoken thought behind it. "Ah, if you know the truth that I do your answer would be important but he does not really believe Grave Digger knows."

173. *"How strangely?"*

Again in an interested way.

179. *"How long will a man lie i'the earth ere he rot?"*

Here Booth somehow conveys the impression that he clearly perceives the uselessness of trying to find out anything from this man, because he had got nothing to tell; that he feels a mild contempt of his stupidity and literal prosaic way of understanding his words; that he thinks best to converse with him about his profession, about things he knows of. Booth asks [179] with a resumption of his tone and manner [in earlier questions] with an added shade of condescension.

195. *"Nay, I know not."*

Spoken in an indifferent and rather heavy tone with an evident effect; his mind is wandering to other matters.

196. *"A pestilence on him for a mad rogue!"*

Laughing immoderately.

200. *"This?"*

Starting up suddenly with an air and tone of great surprise and interest.

Following 201. [Hamlet] Takes the skull.

Holding it up before him in both hands and gazing on it with a strange earnestness shining from his deep, dark, melancholy eyes. You can see his mind going back thro' the long years to the days of his careless childhood and the merry times he had then, contrasting them with the present, and thinking of Yorick's former life and where he is now. A long pause.

201–02. *"Alas, poor Yorick!"*

O the melodious pathos of the "Alas!" and the world of meaning Booth puts into it! The pity and the fondness in his "poor Yorick!"! It seems to me this is the most exquisitely beautiful thing said by Booth. Though it is well-nigh impossible, if not quite so, to select the one from so many fine things. Moonlight again upon his face striking it sidewise; he stands fronting toward left front corner of stage, and at foot of grave.

[1883] Inaudible and far less effective.

202. "I knew him Horatio ..."

Turning to Horatio.

207. "Here hung those lips ..."

Turning back again to the skull. He pats the skull two or three times with his right hand.[3]

215. "... make her laugh at that."

With a faint glimmer of a smile[4] in a tone intensely bitter and sad. From [207 to 216] is all spoken in a dreamy tone and manner as if communing with the skull and Yorick could understand him.

216. "Prithee, Horatio, tell me one thing."

Rousing himself and in a brighter tone, advancing a little.

221. "And smelt so? pah!"

An expression of disgust passes over his face and he takes out his handkerchief and wipes his hands.

223. "To what base uses we may return, Horatio!"

Standing at front center, quite near footlights, and putting his hand on Horatio's shoulder—right hand; they stand facing each other, Horatio towards stage right.

---

3. Clarke does not describe this business. See Shattuck, 257.
4. Although in 1870 Booth seems to have smiled only at 148, in later years, according to Shattuck (255n.6), he played this scene in a more relaxed manner.

230–31. "Alexander died, Alexander was buried, Alexander returneth to dust..."

Removing his hand from Horatio's shoulder Booth lays down his argument, gesticulating with his right hand into palm of left. Being naturally of a speculative turn of mind, he relishes curious researches into the mines of thought, cause and effect, sequences, etc. This train of thought first started by the sight of the Grave Digger and his bones followed indifferently with the unconscious instinct of its usefulness as a needed diversion for his overburdened mind dwelling too constantly on one subject—at last becomes of real interest to him, and as usual when any topic for reflection is mooted he is now determined to follow it out to the end of its intricate windings.

236. "Imperious Caesar, dead and turn'd to clay..."

This improvisation is delivered with considerable animation, to Horatio, Booth facing audience.

240. "But soft! but soft! aside..."

Walking hurriedly towards left corner back of stage, followed by Horatio, and looking in the direction of right corner back where enters funeral procession, which Booth sees at a distance through the church yard and describes at [240–44]; he shades his eyes with his hand.

242. "This doth betoken..."

Addressed partly to Horatio and partly to himself.

245. "Couch we awhile, and mark."

Turning to Horatio and hastily retiring with him to right corner front at end of gravestone nearest footlights, where they stand expectant. Booth with back to audience, left hand on Horatio's shoulder, watching for procession to appear in sight, as from their present station it is invisible. Second Grave Digger enters and lays a rope across grave, out of which clambers First Grave Digger, and waits at a respectful distance.

Immediately on the appearance of the bier in the procession preceded by two attendants bearing torches, Booth uncovers respectfully—i.e., he pushes off the hood of his black fur cloak. So does Horatio.

246. "That is Laertes..."

Turning his face towards Horatio and bestowing on him that familiar tapping; gesture on the breast removing hand from Horatio's shoulder. Not yet does Hamlet suspect whose corpse they bear. Booth then turns his face and body round more towards audience, putting his right hand on Horatio's shoulder down to Horatio's folded arms. Thus they stand listening, respectful spectators, apparently unnoticed and unrecognized by the others who are in middle of stage, absorbed in the funeral rites. Laertes stands at head of grave toward stage left. King and Queen on farther side facing audience. After coffin is lowered the maiden pall-bearers[5] retire to right and left. There are many people grouped around.

265. "What, the fair Ophelia!"

Booth gives a violent start, with his left hand clutches Horatio's arm, glances hastily over his right shoulder towards the grave. Then he throws himself with despairing abandon into Horatio's arms, essaying to put his left arm around Horatio's neck, and burying his face on Horatio's bosom; at the same time Booth sinks down into a sitting posture on end of gravestone. The faithful Horatio receives him affectionately, necessarily bending as Booth sits down, but Horatio remains standing, with his back to audience, and nearly in middle of his shoulders, limp and lifeless, hangs Booth's left hand on which glitters the ring of emerald and diamonds.

267. "I hoped thou shouldst have been my Hamlet's wife..."

That hand is clenched convulsively and tightly, telling a silent tale of heartbreaking agony. Then slowly the fingers unclasp and the hand sways and droops downward, despairingly, with a grace the more exquisite for being so unconscious.

[1883] Booth does on this line what was [in 1881 done later at 269. "O, treble woe..."].

269. "O, treble woe..."

For a moment Booth lifts a ghastly face of agony—on which the moonlight strikes—then he buries it again in Horatio's friendly bosom.

---

5. Booth claimed to be the first American producer to use women pall-bearers. See Shattuck, 259n.9.

272. "Hold off the earth awhile..."

A shudder of emotion runs thro' his frame which shrinks together, and his head droops lower almost it would seem down on to his own right arm on the gravestone, while his left hand rests on the top of Horatio's shoulder, to whom he seems to cling even more closely than before. This is not terror at Laertes's curses, but an added pang of sorrowful surprise at the news of Ophelia's insanity, and remorse that he caused it. No one yet notices the two.

[1883] Booth clenches the hand as before at [267. "I hoped thou ..."] Between [265] "What, the fair Ophelia!" and [277] "What is he whose grief," he lifts a face of ghastly agony, <u>thrice</u>, and the second time he uses his handkerchief as if to wipe away tears; exactly <u>when</u> does he lift his face the second time?[6]

277. "What is he whose grief..."

Beginning to speak with face still bowed and buried and in a choked and shaken voice, gathering as it proceeds a ring of anger.

279. "Conjures the wandering stars ... ?"

Rising slowly with the aid of Horatio.

280–81. "This is I, / Hamlet the Dane."

Wheeling around to face the assembled group, throwing back his head and flinging his cloak backward, brandishing his right arm, and speaking in a tone of mingled dignity, defiance, solemnity and pride.

285. "Yet have I something in me dangerous..."

His eyes roll and glare; he seems choking.

292. "I loved Ophelia..."

Rushing to the foot of the grave and sinking there upon one knee, he gazes into it.

---

6.   Clarke does not describe this business with the handkerchief. See Shattuck, 260–61.

[1883] Booth rushes to foot of grave, kneeling and gazing into it [as before].

292. "... forty thousand brothers ..."

Rising, with arms outspread and lifted heavenward, whither he looks.

[1883] Still kneeling, he spreads his arms and looks heavenward.

293. "Make up my sum."

Turning round he sees Horatio who followed him. [Then] in a paroxysm of grief, Booth throws himself again into Horatio's arms, and for a moment drops his face upon his shoulder.

293. "What wilt thou do for her?"

[1883] Starting up with flashing eyes he glances round and addresses Laertes. He does not go to Horatio again.

297–301. "'Swounds, show me ... leaping in her grave?"[7]

Lashed into a rage by his love and grief, and the shock and the knowledge that he and Ophelia were far dearer to each other than any brother and sister could be.

302. "Be buried quick with her ..."

Pointing into the open grave with left hand.

303–6. "... let them throw ... Make Ossa like a wart!"

Swinging his right arm, and then pointing straight upwards to the sky, stretching himself to his utmost height (reminding me of his Richelieu in the "Curse of Rome" scene) and speaking with great and passionate force.[8]

[1883] Father thinks [these lines] lack the needed passion in Booth's delivery.

---

7. Booth changed "'Swounds" to "Come."

8. This was a particularly striking moment in Booth's performance as Cardinal Richelieu. See Watermeier, "Edwin Booth's Richelieu," 14–15.

Figure 7. John Collier, *Edwin Booth as Cardinal Richelieu,* 1881
This is the point at which Richelieu delivers the "Curse of
Rome" speech.
*(Courtesy of the Hampden-Booth Theatre Library at
The Players, New York City)*

307. "This is mere madness:..."

Booth returns to foot of grave for one last look, standing there with hands clasped and hanging down in front of him.

[1883] Horatio stands behind and near Hamlet. Booth turns to Horatio and in a paroxysm of grief and with that touching manner of appealing to him for help and sympathy stretches out his hands to Horatio—as Richelieu to Joseph, Lear to his Fool—Booth again throws himself into the arms of Horatio who receives him affectionately.

311–12. "Hear you, sir... use me thus?"

With a slightly bewildered air, and in the half grieved, half indignant, and wholly manly tone of one whose feelings have been wounded by a friend.

[1883] Releasing himself from Horatio and addressing Laertes, as [above].

313. "... but it is no matter..."

With a sudden and inexplicable change of tone to that of depicted indifference.

314. "Let Hercules himself do what he may..."

Going out.

319. "... watch over your son."

She signs to an attendant who goes out right.

Scene 2

In Front of the Castle.[9]

[Globe edition V.2.1–236. 236 lines cut to 167]

At 75. Enter Hamlet and Horatio.[10]

---

9. See Shattuck, 265–66 and plate XV, for a description of the 1870 setting for this scene.

10. Booth following traditional practice usually began this scene with line 75, although in his 1870 Booth's Theatre production lines 1–74 were acted. See Shattuck, 267–68 and 268n.16.

Booth has on the fur cloak with hood up. The scene in first grooves and brilliantly lighted.

They enter at right, arm-in-arm, Horatio next to audience, to walk along until [80. "Peace! who comes here?"] where they stand nearly at middle of stage.

Following 80. Enter Osric, L.

Osric is dressed in the height of the fashion in most gaudy style, and is the very extreme top-knot of a gay, young courtier whose obsequious, excessive deference to Hamlet is ludicrous! Booth in middle, half facing Osric who stands at some distance on Booth's left; Horatio stands nearer him on his right.

This scene [with Osric] is the most enjoyable and at the same time heart-rending of the whole play—knowing its antecedents and consequences. Booth's acting is <u>perfectly exquisite</u>, and in no scene in any play is his innate superiority as an actor, his consummate art in trifles, more conspicuous— being at the same time, that wonderful "art which conceals art." This is the scene I should most mourn to miss seeing, or to have "cut out."

Never does Booth look more noble, more handsome, more elegant, graceful, easy—indeed the <u>princeliest</u> Hamlet that ever trod the stage. Beautiful in his serene repose, beautiful the smile which two or three times lights up his fine features as he turns towards Horatio—a smile which vanishes all too quickly. About him still lingers that ineffable melancholy, so deep that no ordinary matter can touch more than the service of his mind, or more transiently. Yet somehow we feel that the terrible pressure of his destiny has slightly lifted from his mind for a brief period and we catch a glimpse of what Hamlet might have been before his mother's second marriage, or father's death; or rather would have been, had the former and the Ghost's visitation not occurred. Booth amuses himself with Osric temporarily; but he treats him with the utmost courtesy, and that peculiarly appropriate courtesy, as from Prince to Courtier. In his last words to Horatio, Booth's voice and face appropriately express the chord of almost heavenly harmony conveyed by the thoughts; while preserving the natural, converstional, friendly manner. "Sweet lord," indeed! and "noble heart"!

For the last time we have seen Hamlet's heart and seen it in affectionate confidential out-pouring with Horatio. A sudden peace and stillness seems to have fallen on the warring elements of Hamlet's soul, the discords of conscience and filial piety inculcating opposite actions, and even on the anguish of his father's murder, etc. Over Booth hovers the spirit of one of

Hamlet's sentences (cut out) "There's a divinity that shapes our ends,/ Rough-hew them how we will" [V.2.10–11]. As the noble form disappears with Horatio going to the well known doom, the impulse to rush upon the stage and prevent it is well night irresistible. Tears unbidden fill our eyes!

The contrast between the serene repose of the true gentleman as exhibited by Booth, and the nervous fidgetiness of the fashionable coxcomb who tries to imitate a gentleman—as exhibited by the actor of Osric—was most edifying, and a perfect exemplification of Hamlet and Osric. Both actors here are equally good, each in his own part. What a pity that the last two scenes are not acted entirely as written by Shakespeare.

82. "I humbly thank you, sir."

Bowing with his own exquisite, princely courtesy, but as a bow of mere politeness, of "noblesse oblige."

83. "Dost know this water-fly?"

Booth evidently considers Osric too frivolous to be worth even his disdain. To prevent Osric's being merely a "bore," Booth plays with him. Booth listens to Osric attentively, but watches him curiously, as if mildly wondering what extravagance the silly creature would act or utter next; he regards him as Gulliver might have done the Lilliputian king; there is also in Booth's manner a hint of the naturalist examining an odd specimen, and an amused questioning that this butterfly should, after all, have the right to be classified a man.

109. "Nay, good my lord; for mine ease, in good faith."

Osric essays to put on his cap then shakes his head, and refuses; he cannot think of putting on his bonnet in the presence of Lord Hamlet! It makes him dreadfully uneasy to think of doing it. Osric keeps bowing and bending, and smiling and squirming, and trying to agree with Hamlet always, in veritable subservience of a courtier. This fawning spirit, Booth always despises; but in Osric it is innocent, so he allows himself to be amused by it, and to be tempted to see how he can lead Osric on, and no deeper feelings are roused. But in case of the manifestation of same spirit by Rosencrantz and Guildenstern, Booth discerns their guilty intentions and feels detestation and repels them.

[At 99. "No, believe me, 'tis very cold" and at 101. "But yet methinks it is very sultry..."], Booth's tone on surface and to Osric sounds sincere as if expressing his actual opinion; so is [145. "I dare not confess..."] spoken apparently in all seriousness. But all about him hovers the amusement. Booth's acting here resembles that in "cloud camel scene" [III.3.392–404] with Polonius. Here the irony seems less blunt, and more light and sportive, and there is no "crazy manner."

141. "What is his weapon?"

Folding his arms quietly and standing in a <u>restful</u> position with one leg thrown a little forward. Such repose and unassuming dignity!

153. "That's two of his weapons..."

Addressed to Osric in a gentle tone of correction.

153. "... but, well."

Meaning "But never mind—go on," waving hand slightly.

158. "... three of the carriages, in faith, are very dear to fancy..."

Osric displays an unbounded, enthusiastic admiration, ridiculously out of proportion to the subject.

162. "What call you the carriages?"

As if he really did not know. Though peerless as a soldier, courtly gentleman, prince and scholar, there are certain court fripperies and fashionable "lingo" of which he may be supposed to be ignorant, his mind was given to matters of more worth, even in his happy youth.

166. "The phrase would be more german to the matter..."

Addressed pointedly to Horatio with an appreciative glance and amused smile. As a general observation which Hamlet cannot avoid making, it is so "apropos," and yet which he scarcely expects Osric to understand or heed—certainly not to answer. Yet it is <u>not</u> a stage "aside" as those [earlier in this scene at 83, 85–86, for example].[11]

---

11.   Lines 83 and 85–86 are marked "aside to Horatio" in the *Prompt Book* edition.

178. "How if I answer 'no'?"

How if I answer—"No"?

180–83. "Sir... 'tis breathing time of day with me..."

The irony is quite dissipated and Booth resumes his natural manner as at [82–83. "I humbly thank you, sir./Dost know this water-fly?"]. Spoken very carelessly and easily with no faintest tint of suspicion that anything is intended but ordinary innocent pastimes on his own part and that of Laertes and King.

So I think this scene must occur at least one day [later], the day after the funeral of Ophelia. Such an affair as a fencing-bout would be quite incongruous for that day. And, morever, the burial on the stage always is represented as taking place at night, or after sunset. Yet this scene always follows immediately the burial, and Booth walks in as if just come from the church yard. Then the fencing match must occur in the evening.

186. "To this effect, sir..."

In tone of this, sleeps the <u>memory</u> of the previous irony!

186–87. "...after what flourish your nature will."

Osric goes almost out, receiving a slight bow from Booth who then approaches to address Horatio. [But then] Osric returns and Booth looks surprised, turning to him.

188. "I commend my duty to your lordship."

In a tone of double-distilled, flattering deference and delight, and finally [he] departs, receiving another bow from Booth, and a slight wave of the hand expressive of a gentle declaration of so much homage.

Following 188. Exit Osric.

Booth and Horatio with a mutual impulse turn towards each other to speak or to confer. It is touching to notice as soon as Osric disappears how Booth's face settles back into its now habitual sadness; the lines relax, showing that an effort had been required to carry on even that trivial conversation with Osric; all the more effort because it was about matters that Hamlet of late had cared nothing for, because it was "trifling." This tension of nerves, and sense of effort when Hamlet is with other people and the subsequent relaxation when left alone, or with Horatio, is sometimes great, sometimes very slight, but the expression of it at the proper time is one of Booth's fine points. He indicates not only the mental, but the corresponding physical condition, and so naturally that it wins appreciative recognition from the "judicious" spectators. A very striking instance is before ["O what a rogue and peasant slave . . ."—II.2.576–634].

219. "I do not think so . . ."

Booth displays a moderate amount of interest in the result of the approaching contest, but speaks with an air of preoccupation and immediately passes to [219–20].

219–20. ". . .since he went into France . . . continual practice . . ."

Horatio's arms are folded, Booth puts his left hand on Horatio's arm and gazes wistfully into his face.

221–22. "But thou wouldst . . . about my heart . . ."

Pressing his right hand to his heart, not in the continental style!

223. ". . . but it is no matter."

Turning his face away from Horatio partly, and towards stage left, and speaking in a tone of trying to throw off a premonition.

224. "Nay, good my lord."

Stepping forward pressing close to Booth, clasping Booth's left hand in his own right and taking Booth's other hand in his own left, I think; speaking in a tone of startled, anxious, lovingness.

225. "It is but foolery . . ."

Tone same as [at 223].

225–26. ". . . but it is such a kind of gain-giving, as would perhaps trouble a woman."

Booth tries to disregard the foreboding by making himself despise it as womanish weakness, but in vain.

227. "If you mind dislike anything, obey it..."

In a decisive tone, with free, friendly offering of services, while the loving anxiety is still preceptible, and his left hand on Booth's right shoulder.

Following 229. "... say you are not fit."

Booth walks toward left as if to go out; Horatio walks along with him, but a step or two behind him, so that although Horatio's back is next to audience, Booth's face and fiqure are plainly visible farther to the left than Horatio's.

230. "Not a whit, we defy augury..."

Spoken in a full, firm voice and brighter tone. Hamlet has conquered the secret dread by bravely looking it in the face, and bidding it defiance, from the calm heights of his imperial reason with the aid of that divine Philosophy whose devoted disciple he has ever been.

230–31. "... there's special providence in the fall of the sparrow."

Both halt; Booth fronts audience.

232–36. "If it be now, 'tis not to come... Let be."

Speaking in a clear, strong, melodious voice, in a sweetly solemn tone, not loudly at all, but most distinctly; addressing Horatio in an easy, unaffected manner, as if he were but breathing out his natural religion. A rare, spiritual expression comes over his countenance, which glows with the "light that never was on land or sea."[12] With the closing words, his face softens into the impression of a benign smile—which yet is not a smile!—and his deep, dark eyes rest upon Horatio's face seeming to say, "My friend! There's a divinity that shapes our ends, rough-hew them how we will. Trust!"

235. "... leave betimes?"

Both resume their walk, and, I think, Booth slips his arm into Horatio's.

---

12. William Wordsworth, "Elegiac Stanzas Suggested by a Picture of Peele Castle" (1805).

236. "Let be."

Said just before they disappear and with exquisite gentleness, and perhaps as a reply to some additional expostulation from Horatio, either of word, or look, or gesture, perceived by Booth only.

Scene 3

A Hall in the Castle.[13]

[Globe edition V.2.237–414. 178 lines cut to 98]

Thrones on which are seated King and Queen are at center back. Queen left, Osric on right. Horatio is on left at the end of table where there stands foils. All except sovereigns are standing. We miss Polonius from his usual station at King's right hand. Courtiers and attendants are numerous. Booth's manner to King is, as usual on state occasions and in presence of the assembled court, polite, but cold. Yet he shows less marked aversion and avoidance of conversing with him than in [Act I].

Booth wears his house cloak with bare head, the one with hood. He has thrown off the fur cloak worn over this one before entering Scene 3.

[1883] Booth enters with Horatio from left and advances to meet Laertes at center. Booth wears the same fur cloak as in previous scene, but the hood is thrown off. They shake hands cordially.

237. "Come, Hamlet, come, and take this hand from me."

That is, the hand of Laertes.

238. "Give me your pardon, sir..."

Booth takes Laertes cordially by the hand and bows over it and speaks in sincerity. They stand in middle and turn as to face the throne.

263. "I embrace it freely."[14]

---

13. Following 236, Booth changed the scene for his Act V.3. The court was discovered and then Hamlet and Horatio made their entrance. See Shattuck, 273–74, for a description of the 1870 setting for this scene. As Shattuck notes (274n.23), however, as early as 1873, Booth had reverted to a setting very similar, if not identical, to the setting for I.2—"a Room of State."

14. Booth cut a considerable number of lines in Hamlet's apology and Laertes's response 238–63. See Shattuck, 281, for a listing of the cuts for this scene.

Booth has continued to hold the hand of Laertes and now again presses it cordially.

[1883] Booth casts his left arm with careless affection around Laertes' neck as they both turn to face the throne and bow slightly to King.

265. "Give us the foils."

Dropping Laertes' hand and walking off towards table at left.

[1883] Walking off to table at left.

265. "Come, one for me."

[1883] On removing his heavy fur cloak which he casts upon the table, I think, Booth at last appears in the familiar black tunic with its narrow purple belt and tassels, and his long black stockings—which are <u>not</u> laced with ribbon as before.

266–71. "I'll be your foil, Laertes... Very well, my lord."

[1883] Somewhere between [these lines] is the following new and striking "bit of business." Booth takes from his bosom the locket containing the miniature of his beloved father, looks at it, kisses it fervently, and then removing the chain from which it is suspended from his own neck hangs it around Horatio's and commits the precious token to his friend's keeping.[15] Knowing how soon Hamlet's death is to occur, this action assumes a touching significance in the eye of the spectator. How much Horatio must have valued that last gift from his "dear lord"! Spreads his handkerchief on arm of an armchair near table.

269. "No, by this hand."

Holding out to Laertes his right hand. And truly Booth speaks with entire sincerity, utterly without irony.

271. "Very well, my lord."

Taking the foil.

---

15. Clarke does not describe this business. See Shattuck, 275. See also line 363 below.

Following 274. "... we have therefore odds."

Hamlet and Horatio appear to consult each other as to the quality of the foil.

276. "This likes me well."

Handling the foil to try it.

279. "If Hamlet give the first or second hit..."

Booth stands with back to audience and rapier in right hand, apparently finding that the white ruching at wrist interferes with the free handling of his weapon, he busies himself diligently with tucking it away up his sleeve.[16]

280. "Or quit in answer to the third exchange..."

This treacherous speech makes one shudder.

[1883] He faces audience this time while tucking away ruching at wrist, and then, after brandishing his foil, walks down stage towards footlights to meet Laertes who advances from right and both take position at center front facing throne.

286. "And let the kettle to the trumpet speak..."

King stands. Laertes also "salutes" King at same time with Hamlet.

289. "'Now the king drinks to Hamlet.'"

Booth "salutes" the King with his rapier in military form.

293. "Stay; give me drink."

They are just resuming fencing, but check themselves, drop their rapiers and bow deferentially.

293. "Hamlet, this pearl is thine..."

---

16. Clarke does not describe this business here or at line 280 below. See Shattuck, 275–76.

King pretends to drop a pearl into the cup.

294. "Give him the cup."

Bernardo carries cup to Hamlet on a salver; then at [295. "... set it by awhile"] sets it on small round table at Queen's left hand.

296. "Come." [They play.]

As Hamlet and Laertes fence, they occupy foreground and center of stage moving quickly back and forth. Booth has his face to audience and holds his left arm, as if to balance himself, upper half at rights angles with body, lower half at right angles with upper half, the wrist and hand bent slightly inwards—and odd fashion, but like all his attitudes, graceful.

Booth fences beautifully and skillfully, with full, squared shoulders front to audience. Laertes has his back generally to audience. Booth's face appears flushed and he seems a little excited and considerably interested in the fencing, an interest which increases with his successful hits. He looks young and handsome, seems good humored, almost cheerful, and after each "bout" eager for Laertes to come on again. He plays with an innocent heartiness which serves to make the poorer fencing of his opponent appear to be the forced playing of a treacherous man whose secret designs oppress him.[17]

Following 296. "... what say you?"

With a bright smile and in a tone of friendly triumph.

301. "Good madam!"

"Saluting" his mother.

307. "And yet 'tis almost 'gainst my conscience."

[1883] Laertes stands at right front corner.

309. "I pray you, pass with our best violence..."

In a bright cheerful tone of friendly challenge.

---

17. Compare Clarke's description of the fencing match in Shattuck, 276–77.

[1883] Booth walks across left center towards Laertes.

311. "Say you so? come on."

In a tone in which there lurks a threat; like "Ha! You think so, do you? You shall soon find out that I am not trifing with you!"

315. "How is it, my lord?"

Booth stands in the middle of stage, back to throne, he reels a little, shuts his eyes, makes a sort of hissing moan, as one does at a sudden, stinging, smarting wound, and puts his hand to his chest, Horatio rushes toward him to help him, tries to undo his tunic while his tone expresses surprised curiosity. Booth appears only slightly hurt, "a mere scratch," and is not much overcome. From [where Laertes wounds Hamlet] the action and speeches are very rapid to [322] so that everything seems to happen at once, as it were, and so suddenly as to startle and appall everyone and leave no time for reflection.

316. "How is 't, Laertes?"

Laertes is taken care of by Osric at right.

318. "How does the queen?"

Booth puts his hand upon Horatio, and probably attracted by the stir around the Queen or her moans, he turns partly round and asks in a tone of astonishment and charm, meaning "What is the matter with the Queen?" while he faces towards Queen.

322. "O, villainy!"

In reply to his mother's appeal [320–21. "O, my dear Hamlet,/The drink... I am poisoned."] in a tone of astonishment, distress, and condemnation. Booth stands in center of stage with his back to audience.

324. "Ho! Let the door be lock'd: Treachery! Seek it out!"

Waving his right arm with his rapier, and speaking in a loud voice with a tone of decisive command.[18]

---

18. Shattuck (277n.29) notes that Booth never used the business of exchanging rapiers, although he included the Folio direction "In scuffling they change rapiers" in the

302. "Hamlet, thou art slain;..."

Booth turns round and approaches Laertes with an air of bewilderment, and crouching in front of Laertes listens to his words as if trying to understand what has happened and what is the meaning of this terrible tragedy—a triple tragedy in the midst of an innocent fencing-bout. Booth has been stunned by the suddenness and horror of the stabbing, the poisoning, etc., by the treachery so unexpected by his generous heart, and cannot imagine why Laertes stabbed him in the first place, though when it occurred he naturally defended himself.

326. "In thee there is not half an hour of life."

Horatio stands close beside Hamlet, as if to be ready for any emergency, with his hand on Hamlet's left arm and listening eagerly to what Laertes is saying. Horatio's alarm and grief are manifest. But Booth pays little heed to the news of his fatal injury; he is not frightened for <u>himself</u> but earnestly eager for further explanation or the whole matter. His mouth is open, and eyes seem starting from their sockets.

332. "The point envenom'd too!"

Booth glares upon the sword in his hand—which is the one Laertes used in fencing—touches the blade, half realizing for the first time that Laertes played the "bouts" with him with a sharp and dangerous sword—and that it was poisoned too! Laertes murdering and murdered, his mother poisoned,—and "the King, the King's to blame." Hamlet apprehends the facts, discerns that it was all a planned treachery, but there is no time nor mood for reflection. As by an electric flash, his mind sees the past crimes of the King, his wicked propensity to continue to commit them—as shown by the present scene—and the sense of his own imminent death makes it "Now or never!" that he must act.

333. "Then, venom, to thy work."

Over Booth's face sweeps a <u>lurid flame</u> of <u>determination</u>, and gripping his sword, he still crouching, <u>whirls around towards his left hand</u>, then, rising, strides swiftly towards the throne.

---

the *Prompt Book* edition. Usually Booth seems to have kept *both* rapiers down to 332, but Stone clearly indicates that Booth had only one rapier and thus must have effected the exchange.

Following 334. "Treason! treason!"[19]

The resolute impetuosity of Hamlet's onslaught is irresistible. Even Horatio is pushed aside, and lords and courtiers with their drawn swords are scattered right and left. The King has risen to his feet. Straight up the steps of the throne Booth rushes to the King and stabs him. The King reels and staggers backward down the steps.

336–38. "Here, thou incestuous, murdrous, damned Dane … Follow my mother."

Booth leaps into his place, fronting the audience, and stabs the King again and to death. So, at last, is done the deed of vengeance to which Hamlet has so long been called, as to a holy duty, by his father's spirit. In the final impulse, perhaps his aim was chiefly served by the pang of the thought that his mother had been poisoned by the King—for Hamlet never knows that this was accidental.

Following 338. The King falls and dies.

King lies on floor between throne and large table at left; Bernardo bends over him.

Following 342. "Nor thine on me!" [Laertes dies.]

Horatio has followed Hamlet to the foot of the throne excited by sympathy with Hamlet in his action, while his heart is wrung with anxiety, love and grief, at the thought of Hamlet's rapidly approaching death.

343. "Heaven make thee free of it!"

Booth slowly bows his head towards Laertes and speaks in a tone of solemn forgiveness.

344. "I am dead, Horatio."

Booth steps down a little to meet Horatio, who setting one foot on the lowest step of the throne, stretches up his arms to Hamlet, while Booth

---

19.   The direction in the *Prompt Book* edition at this point is "Lords draw their swords to defend the King. Hamlet rushes through the crowd and stabs him."

turns to Horatio and reaches down his hands to him. Booth makes a tone and gesture expressive of such a wealth of love and confidence, of certainty of his sympathy, and reliance upon his manliness to act for justice after he has gone, that a reflex mantle of these qualities is thrown over the actor playing Horatio. Now Booth begins to feel the effects of the poison, shown by his staggering limbs and failing voice. His profile is given to audience. Both at corner of dais next stage left. Booth seems quietly sinking down.

Following 353. "Here's yet some liquor left."[20]

With his right hand from the little round table. It is a curiously shaped gold goblet.

[1883] The chief difference I notice is that Booth moves his sword and shows more sense of triumph after stabbing the King. And then he sinks down into King's chair on throne dais. At ["Here's yet some liquor left"] wresting away the cup is done the same; only all the action and the death occurs at summit of dais instead of on the steps of throne.

353. "As thou 'rt a man..."

Booth rouses himself with an instinct to save his dear friend, "the good Horatio" from death, into whose terrible cyclone, just raging, so many have been sucked. He has no cold, calculating desire of preserving Horatio for his own future fame. (Scorned even be the thought, and may it perish with that other foul suggestion that Hamlet at last kills the King in revenge for the latter's treacherous designs against his own life!!) Booth at first conjures and beseeches Horatio, then commands; and then making the last desperate and evidently tremendous effort of a dying man, he struggles with Horatio, wrests the cup from him, and flings it far over Horatio's head into the "wings" at stage left.

355. "O, good, Horatio, what a wounded name..."

---

20. The *Prompt Book* edition reads "Seizes the cup. Hamlet wrests it from him." Clarke describes the action as follows: "Horatio seeing the poisoned cup, which has been left on the table at the left, runs to it and snatches it; and coming halfway back towards Hamlet offers to drink it. Hamlet looks up commandingly! ... Starting up, he runs to Horatio and grasps the cup ... He wrenches the cup from Horatio and throws it off stage left. He falls to his knees with Horatio supporting him." See Shattuck (279n.31) for Booth's changes in staging this action after 1870.

Horatio overcome with despairing grief, bows his head upon his arm. Booth and Horatio still cling affectionately to each other. This [line] is spoken in tone and manner partly as if in apologetic explanation of his wresting away the cup, and thus frustrating what was evidently the earnest wish of Horatio's heart, partly as if for the purpose of dissuading Horatio from attempting suicide again. To accomplish the latter, Hamlet, chiefly for Horatio's sake, and not for his own, appeals to what he knows will be an all powerful motive, rooted as it is in Horatio's love and devotion for himself, and conjures Horatio not to die for his sake, but to live and suffer for his sake, and all this in a tone which fully appreciates Horatio's grief. Of course, Hamlet feels also the natural and noble desire to leave a reputation after his death in true accordance with his life; but this is secondary with him, I insist. The case resembles that in French history when Napoleon before battle of Austerlitz stimulated the bravery of his soldiers by promising to keep his adored person safely out of fire so long as they fought with such vigor as to insure the defeat of the enemy. All the time Booth's trembling limbs, occasionally gasping utterance, and increasing pallor, etc. show that death is near. He writhes a little, and the hand placed upon Horatio, as a caress, lingers there with the clutch for bodily support. The voluntary expressions of emotion, usually so varied and so beautiful on his wonderfully mobile face, are now contending with the involuntary contortions of bodily distress (though the latter are not exaggerated) and both seem to fade away together.

363. "O, I die, Horatio . . ."

This is as touching as the cry made by a very sick little child for its mother's hand! Booth staggers a little away from Horatio and slowly fronts the audience, but still clinging closely to Horatio's hand with both of his. Horatio presses forward to support him with his right arm, half bending his knees while pierced with anguish to see stamped upon the features of his beloved friend that awful look which most of us so well remember on the face of some dear one, which tells the stricken heart that Death has come to claim his own. The ashen hue, and strange cavernous look of the dying, is seen upon Booth's face, the indrawn eyes, and the pinched look about the mouth, while the lines of his face settle into rigidity. His eyes do not roll up at all, but slowly, slowly the eyelids open wider and wider, and in their sunken depths life lingers latest as he gazes steadily before him; while for a moment you seem to catch a gleam of the immortal soul whose thoughts do wander darkly through eternity. Then comes the stare of vacancy, his frame totters and sinks, his eyelids droop, and his head falls slowly forward on his breast. While from his white lips fall the whispered words "the rest is silence," and a courtier from stage right springs forward with extended arms to support sides of Booth opposite to Horatio.

To the last Booth keeps hold of Horatio's hand and his last thoughts given to any human being are evidently bestowed upon Horatio. You can see just the second when the breath leaves his body, by the sudden slight drop downwards into limp lifelessness, and 'tis the head of a corpse which touches the steps of the throne at last, gently let down by friendly hands.

[1883] [Between "O, I die, Horatio" and 364. "The potent poison quite o'ercrows my spirit"] Horatio lifts from his own breast the locket containing the miniature of Hamlet's father and holds it before the eyes fast glazing in death. A bright look of recognition, that struggles to form a smile, gleams for an instant on Booth's face.

369. "The rest is silence."

Is quite inaudible, but you see the lips move. There is less front view of the dying Hamlet afforded.

370. "Good night, sweet prince…"

And poor Horatio kneeling by his side and pressing the cold hands never before unresponsive to his loving clasp!

371. "And flights of angels sing thee to thy rest!"[21]

Horatio looks heavenward.

This death-scene sounds long in the description, but on the stage seems by no means so. There is no theatrical, protracted exhibition of death-throes and long drawn-out failing; but all is done quietly and naturally, with sufficient indication of physical suffering to excite pity without disgust. Watching in breathless suspense, you long to check the too swiftly ebbing sands of that noble life.

21. Booth ended the play with this line.

Booth's Iago and Othello

Figure 8. Thomas Hicks, *Edwin Booth as Iago,* 1863
Booth varied his costuming as Iago considerably during his
career (see figs. 9–11).
*(Courtesy of the National Portrait Gallery, Smithsonian
Institution, Washington, D.C.)*

Act I

Scene 1

Venice. A Dark Street. Full Stage.[1]

[Globe edition I.1.1–184. 184 lines cut to 124]

Enter Roderigo and Iago.

Iago [wears] light brown tights, brown leather low boots with leather straps laced around half way to the knees, light brown tunic jacket with scarlet sleeves and scarlet trimmings, gold necklace lying over the jacket; elegant scarlet hat with a white plume and scarlet plumes—most becoming shape—black and white checked cloak; a black belt studded with jewels. From his larger necklace hangs a dagger in a case. Black moustache and small pointed beard.

[1884] Light gray plush tunic with scarlet silk collar laid back from a low neck open to show linen shirt. Pointed hood behind lined with the same scarlet silk, bearing a small gray silk tassel at the point. Sleeves of gray plush

---

1. Booth's 1869 production of *Othello* at Booth's Theatre had fifteen scenically spectacular sets. Unfortunately, unlike his productions of *Hamlet* and *Richelieu*, no renderings of these settings have survived. However, after he lost his theatre and was solely a touring star, he generally, except for the Booth-Barrett tours in the late 1880s, had to be content with much simpler scenic arrangements. *Othello* #67 indicates a ground-plan much like the setting Stone describes, as does the "Benson Sherwood Stage Plans and Settings of Scenery for Plays at Booth's Theatre, 1873–83 and at the Fifth Avenue Theatre, 1878–87" manuscript in the collection of the New York Public Library at Lincoln Center. Both of these sources describe a setting consisting of a series of "Italian Street" flats and a "Set house" with a balcony door and window that was placed diagonally upstage right. In any case, perhaps because it lacked distinction, Stone only occasionally remarks on the scenery.

Figure 9.   Photograph of Booth as Iago
*(Courtesy of the Hampden-Booth Theatre Library at
The Players, New York City)*

gathered and looped up considerably above elbow, leaving undersleeves of scarlet silk quite tight fitting trimmed with gilt buttons and having white ruching around wrists. The tunic is trimmed with a scarlet tassels.

Roderigo [wears] a rich green velvet tunic-jacket trimmed with glittering gold fringe, black hat with white plume. He is light complexioned, light hair and pink skin—a contrast to Booth as Iago.

93. "Most reverend signior, do you know my voice?"

Iago stands at right of stage by corner of Brabantio's house, not exactly under the window; while Roderigo, out in the street in front of window, talks to Brabantio. Iago's attitude is easy and graceful.[2]

119. "You are—a senator."

Iago steps forward towards the window, doffing his plumed hat and making an obeisance of satirical reverence to Brabantio.

[1884] "You are" is spoken angrily, starting forward as if to resent [i.e., to show resentment] by some bodily attack on Brabantio, the application to himself of such an epithet. "A senator" with tone of satirical reverence as above, but without the obeisance, a tone which somehow suggests that Iago thinks it impolitic to quarrel with Brabantio.

155. "Though I do hate him as I do hell pains..."

Hateful expression.

159. "Lead to the Sagittary the raised search..."

Booth pronounced in three syllables "Sag-i-tare."

Scene 2

Venice. The Sagittary. Second Grooves.

[Globe edition I.2. 99 lines cut to 90]

Act I. Othello's Dress. White gown, draped on side with green and silver

---

2. Booth's note in the *Variorum* (19) is: "Brabantio should be seen through the open window at his book or papers; this would account for his appearance, instead of his servants, at the 'terrible summons.' Iago should keep in the shadow during this." References are to page numbers in the *Variorum*.

Figure 10. Booth as Othello: "Keep up your bright swords . . ."
(I.2.59)
Wood engraving by W. J. Hennessy.
*(Courtesy of the Hampden-Booth Theatre Library at
The Players, New York City)*

jewels. Light green satin vest, gold buttons, gold undersleeves; sash of light green silk very broad and swathed around waist, ends in front with pale pink fringe. Diamond and emerald rings. Sword in sash on right side with spendid hilt. Necklace of steely silver; earrings large and flashy like diamonds. Small purple velvet turban-like cap trimmed with gold lace. White stockings with light green velvet or satin high heeled shoes trimmed with gold lace. Necklace consists of large ovals, each made of a solid ruby set in brilliants, and linked with a pearl to its neighbor.[3]

81. "Subdue him at his peril."

Cassio and Iago and their soldiers draw their swords as if to defend Othello from arrest; the others draw also.

82. "Both you of my inclining, and the rest..."

They drop swords and sheathe them, Iago with a peculiarly graceful deference to Othello.[4]

Scene 4

The Council Chamber. The Duke of Venice and the Senators are discovered Right with a Messenger kneeling before them. Enter as the scene opens, Gratiano, Ludovico and Paulo.

[Globe edition I.3.33–301. 268 lines cut to 220][5]

---

3. This description taken from Stone's separate notes on Booth's performance as Othello.

4. Booth's note in the *Variorum* (41) is: "Now Othello's friends draw. Othello stands between the two parties with sheathed scimetar held up; its crescent shape lends a little Oriental atmosphere to the picture. 'Tis harmless."

5. Booth divided I.3 of the Globe edition into at least two and sometimes three scenes as follows, exclusive of internal line cuts: I.3.1–32, I.4 (Globe I.3.33–301) and I.5 (Globe I.3.302–410). In earlier productions, he staged I.3.1–32, but later in his career he omitted these lines. The *Prompt Book* edition, for example, generally prints the lines with the note that "Scene Third is sometimes omitted." Booth changed the settings for each of the scenes staged. Booth's I.3, for example, was set in the "Anteroom of the Council Chamber." Stone noted that in 1880, Booth's I.3 was "acted," but omitted in the 1881 and 1884 performances she observed. On I.3 she commented only that "Gratiano wears a large purple cloak." When Booth staged I.3 he assigned the Duke's lines to Gratiano, the First Senator's lines to Lodovico, and the Second Senator's lines to Paulo.

Duke wears ducal coronet and is seated on dais with senators around him on dais also; steps leading up to it, and a vacant chair for Brabantio.[6]

Following 47. Enter Brabantio, Othello, Iago, Roderigo and Officers.

Othello, Cassio, and officers stand on left opposite Duke. Iago and Roderigo stand at back of stage, left center, dressed as in the first scene, Iago with his hand on Roderigo's shoulder, leaning gracefully, their hats in their hands. Iago's face is quiet, calm, reserved, and handsome; he watches and listens to Othello, occasionally exchanging a whispered remark with Roderigo of evidently trivial importance.

[1884] Booth does not, this time, look quite so free and easy and as it were innocent, as usual. Though his attitude is calm and quiet, his face, espec-ially those glittering eyes, show the keen plotting soul, alert in watch-fulness of everybody's word or action, if perchance he can take any advantage of it. This is especially noticeable after the entrance of Desdemona [following 176].

120. "Even fall upon my life."

About this time, Brabantio takes his seat on the dais and bows his head in grief.

121. "Ancient, conduct them; you best know the place."

Iago starts forward, gracefully moves his hand slightly, makes that peculiar and wonderfully expressive slight inclination of deference (which is Booth's own and inimitable) and goes out, putting on his hat as he disap-pears at left center back.

128–70. "Her father loved me ... let her witness it."[7]

Othello stands in middle of stage in front of dais.

---

6. The ground plan in *Othello* #67 indicates the dais was placed down right with the senators seated at long tables above the dais. Booth's note in the *Variorum* (47) is: "The Duke should be busy with papers or conferring with the senators, while Brabantio takes his seat; which will account for his 'I did not see you'" [line 50].

7. Booth's note in the *Variorum* (54) on this famous speech is: "All this as modestly as possible,—not a breath of bluster, and not declamatory; *very* difficult to render natu-rally. The Duke and senators, indeed all present, should listen with rapt attention."

Following 169. "This only is the witchcraft I have used..."

[Roderigo] enters at left center back of stage.

170. "Here comes the lady; let her witness it."

Brabantio rises and steps down and stands at right of stage, as he addresses Desdemona [178–80].

Following 176. "If she confess that she was half the wooer..."

Desdemona enters at left center, and stands in middle of stage.

179. "Do you perceive in all this noble company... ?"[8]

Iago and Roderigo resume their [former stage] positions.

180–89. "My noble father... the Moor my lord."

During Desdemona's speech, [Othello] looks at her eagerly with dilating eyes, expressing joy at her devotion and eagerness for her petition to be answered favorably.[9]

192–95. "Come hither, Moor... For your sake, jewel."[10]

[1884] Iago is especially attentive and exhibits emotion here.[11]

220. "I humbly beseech you, proceed to the affairs of state."

---

8. The *Prompt Book* edition indicates that Iago entered after 178 ("Light on the man ...") with Desdemona. The direction reads: "Enter Desdemona, attended by two Ladies, Iago, and Officers."

9. This description is taken from Stone's separate notes on Booth's performance as Othello.

10. Booth cut 195b–219 except for 198, "I have done, my lord."

11. Booth's note in the *Variorum* (67) on line 222 may help clarify Stone's comment: "Othello leaves Desdemona with Cassio, who regards her with tender yet respectful admiration. Iago, at back, watches them curiously, but let him not be obtrusive; he must keep in the background and assume this expression, and feel the curiousness, even if only one person in the whole audience sees or understands it; the 'censure,' as Hamlet calls it, of that one is worth all the rest."

Brabantio reseats himself.

260. "By his dear absence. Let me go with him."

Iago manifests a slight start of surprise and pleasure. Is it possible that Booth intends to indicate that Iago has a personal predilection already for Desdemona?[12]

293. "Look to her, Moor, if thou hast eyes to see…"

[1884] Iago by a start and a malicious look shows that he takes heed of this remark and you remember the future use he makes of it [in III.3.206–8]. Notice the difference in the bearing of Iago when with Othello, with Roderigo, and again when alone when the depths of his natural villainy are revealed. Shakespeare shows this by the words put into Iago's mouth, so far as printed words can; Booth shows it by tone, manner, looks, etc.

295. "My life upon her faith! Honest Iago…"

Othello embracing Desdemona. Iago advances. Similar to [his earlier movement at 121].

Following 301. Exeunt Othello and Desdemona. Change.[13]

Scene 5

A Dark Street. First Grooves.

[Globe edition I.3.302–410. 108 lines cut to 81]

Enter Iago and Roderigo. Dressed as in the first scene. Iago has on light brown woolen gauntlet-gloves, nicely fitting and very effective with his rakish-looking hat.

---

12. Stone then refers herself—and future readers—to Iago's soliloquy. II.1.295–321.

13. In the *Prompt Book* edition, Booth indicated that Iago and Roderigo exited following 298 ("And bring them after in the best advantage") and then re-entered following the scene change. *Othello* #67 indicates, however, that everybody exited following 300 except Iago and Roderigo. Since Booth's I.4 was set on the full stage and his I.5 in the "First Grooves," Iago and Roderigo might have been enclosed by the new setting, entering through it immediately after the change was effected. Apparently this was the action Stone observed since she indicates that there was a change of scene here with everyone exiting except Iago and Roderigo. Undoubtedly the setting was a reduced version of the "Italian Street" scene used in I.1.

[1884] No gloves at all this time.

307. "If thou dost, I shall never love thee after. Why, thou silly gentle-man!"[14]

Laughing.

311–16. "O villainous! . . . to love himself."

[1884] Walking up near Roderigo on his right side. Villainous laughter [after 315–16. "I never found man that knew how to love himself," and again after 318. "I would change my humanity with a baboon"].

322–23. "Virtue! a fig! 'tis in ourselves that we are thus or thus."[15]

Pointing up and then down.

340–41. "Come, be a man! Drown thyself! drown cats and blind puppies."

Patting him on the shoulder.

365. "A pox of drowning thyself!"[16]

[1884] Turning away from Roderigo, walking off towards right corner front.

371. "Thou art sure of me: go, make money . . ."

[1884] Going back from right corner front, close up to Roderigo.

373. "I hate the Moor . . ."

[1884] With great emphasis, earnestness.

375. "Let us be conjunctive in our revenge against him . . ."

---

14. Booth's notes in the *Variorum* (81) is: "Tapping him playfully on the forehead."
15. Booth cut a considerable number of Iago's lines in this and his next speech, including 323b–340a, part of 346—"defeat thy favor with an usurped beard"—and 353–62.
16. Booth substituted "plague" for "pox."

Shaking hands with Roderigo.

[1884] Locking arms with Roderigo on Roderigo's right side and sort of snuggling up to him with an indescribable air of confidential plotting of wickedness.

379. "Traverse! go, provide thy money."

[1884] Walking away again and walking up and down on right side of stage.

385. "Go to; farewell."

Roderigo is going out towards left.

385. "Do you hear, Roderigo?"

Standing still, facing towards Roderigo who is going out.

387. "No more of drowning, do you hear?"

Laughing.

388. "I am changed..."

[1884] Roderigo exits left.

389. "Thus do I ever make my fool my purse..."

[1884] Advancing towards footlights near middle of stage front.

392. "I hate the Moor."

[1884] Pulling off his hat.

396. "Will do as if for surety."

Shakes his gauntleted fist.

400. "In double knavery—How, how?—Let's see:—"

[1884] Pulling a forelock down towards his eyebrows.

401–4. "After some time ... framed to make women false."

At first Iago seems to be cogitating and thinking hard; at "After some time ... " the vague ideas evidently take shape in his brain, as indicated by a look of ugly exultation.

[1884] This look reminds of the expression of face in <u>Little Dorrit</u> whose "nose went down and his moustache came up."[17]

408. "As asses are."

Said with great contempt.

409. "I have't. It is engender'd!"

[1884] Clutching his forehead.

410. "Must bring this monstrous birth to the world's light."

[Iago exits] left.

---

17. "When Monsieur Rigaud laughed, a change took place in his face, that was more remarkable than preposessing. His moustache went up under his nose, and his nose came down over his moustache, in a very sinister and cruel manner." Charles Dickens, *Little Dorrit* (1857). See Oxford University Press edition (1979), Book I, chapter 1, 7.

Act II

*Famagusta, a Fortified Sea-Port Town in the Island of Cyprus. Castle on
Platform right. Seaview center. Stone Seat center. Platform and Steps at
Back Arch Left. The Scene is in Front of the Castle, at Sunset. Cassio,
Montano and Several Gentlemen Discovered.*[1]

[Globe edition II.1.1–321, II.2.1–14, and II.3.1–394. 729 lines cut to 506]

[1884] A beautiful mountain is seen not far off across the harbor, a gorgeous
crimson light fills the atmosphere and shines on the faces and armor, very
beautiful and odd, but not much resembling a sunset.[2] Cassio wears a wine-
colored velvet tunic-jacket.

[Globe edition II.1]

65. "Does tire the ingener."[3]

[1884] Iago conducts Desdemona forward to Cassio and there leaves her
with a curious gesture, as if he carelessly tossed her off.

97. Good ancient, you are welcome.

---

1. Booth played the three scenes of the Globe edition Act II as one scene in a single
   setting. The Herald's proclamation (II.2.1–14) was "sometimes omitted" as the *Prompt
   Book* edition notes, but Stone wrote that it was "acted every time I've seen Booth." It
   has been deleted in an 1868 Booth prompt book (*Othello* #59), but retained in all
   others. Booth cut II.1.1–42, beginning the scene with Cassio's speech 43–46.

2. A Booth prompt book (*Othello* #65) has the following note. "Time: near Sunset. Red
   medium or calcium on and during scene turns to Green. Calcium (fire) L. on castle."
   The ground plan in *Othello* #67 refers to the "Island of Cyprus drop." See also notes
   for the settings to Acts III and IV below.

3. Booth replaced this phrase with "Does bear all excellency?"

Iago at left of stage, who acknowledges his greeting with a courteous inclination.

101. "Sir, would she give you so much of her lips..."

[1884] At this point, it seems to me Booth begins his extra-fine acting. The power of his voice for expressing sarcasm in all its varied shades is perfectly marvellous. And so is the perfect <u>naturalness</u> of his manner of speaking.

106. "Marry, before your ladyship, I grant..."

[1884] Bowing slightly and respectfully to Desdemona.

107. "She puts her tongue a little in her heart..."

[1884] Touching his heart with right hand.

109. "Come on, come on; you are pictures out of doors..."

[1884] Iago saunters easily up and down at left front corner of stage near a stone pillar.

112. "Saints in your injuries, devils being offended..."

[1884] Clasping his hands as if saying his prayers, but in a mocking way.

117. "No, let me not."[4]

[1884] O, the sneering tone in which this is uttered! And the bitter smile! He faces the audience.

119. "O gentle lady, do not put me to't..."

[1884] Turning toward Desdemona and addressing her with the utmost deference. You receive the impression that during the voyage Iago has made himself most agreeable to Desdemona, and that they have become much more familiarly acquainted; yet no intimation of anything not perfectly proper.

---

4. Booth's note in the *Variorum* (107) is: "Linger on 'no' with a significant side glance at her. All that he says till he speaks 'aside' [168–69] should be delivered humorously, to conceal his bitterness, which his features occasionally reveal."

122. "Ay, madam."[5]

Cassio appears to be the one addressed, and he certainly is the one who answers, and <u>not</u> Iago.

123–24. "... but I do beguile/The thing I am, by seeming otherwise."[6]

Desdemona addresses the one who answered, until at [145. "But what praise ... ?"] she turns again to Iago and addresses <u>him</u>.

126. "I am about it; but indeed my invention/Comes from my pate..."

Iago rubs his forehead as a man does naturally who is trying to think of something.

158. "See suitors following and not look behind..."

[1884] He is facing audience and casts a slight glance over his right shoulder, as if hinting at an invitation of her whom he is describing.

161. "To suckle fools and chronicle small beer."

Bowing low to Desdemona.

168. "He takes her by the palm..."

Leaning against a low stone pillar at left of stage.

180. "The Moor! I know his trumpet."

Stepping forward towards center and putting on his hat, as do the other men, to be ready to doff them to Othello.

---

5. This line is usually Iago's, but Booth's note in the *Variorum* (107) is: "Cassio should make this reply. He has been awaiting their arrival. Iago has just landed with Desdemona." Although the line is assigned to Iago in the *Prompt Book* edition, in all of Booth's extant working prompt books, it is assigned to Cassio.

6. Booth cut Desdemona's line 125; then he transposed her speech 145–48 to the end of 124. He also cut 130–44, so that Iago's response to Desdemona included 126–29 and 149–59.

*Following 182. Enter Othello and Attendants C. Iago, Cassio and Gentle-
men salute Othello.*[7]

Othello dressed in steel armor.

202–4. "O, you are well tuned now!... As <u>honest</u> as I am."[8]

Leaning against same low pillar at left of stage and wearing a villainous
expression. The concentrated sarcasm with which his voice is filled is
wonderful!

[1884] Spontaneous applause from audience.

206. "How does my old acquaintance of this isle?"

Shaking hands with Montano.

209. "In mine own comforts. I prithee, good Iago..."

Iago starts forward from left with gesture of obedience.

214. "Once more, well met at Cyprus."

Embracing her as they go out.

223. "Lay thy finger thus, and let thy soul be instructed."[9]

Iago stands at Roderigo's left side.

258. "Blessed fig's-end!"

[1884] Snapping his fingers.

258–59. "... the wine she drinks is made of grapes..."

---

7. Booth cut Cassio's lines 181 and 183.
8. Stone also put quotation marks around the word "honest" to indicate how much Booth
    emphasized the word.
9. Booth cut 229–55.

Looking straight at Roderigo.

264. "Lechery, by this hand..."[10]

Holding out his right hand close to Roderigo's face. He stands now close up to Roderigo with that peculiar intimate, trusting way which Booth employs to indicate confidential plotting; he does it with his whole body and tone, not any specific gestures.

295. "That Cassio loves her, I do well believe't..."

[1884] Sits down on seat in center by stone pillar.

296. "That she loves him 'tis apt and of great credit..."

[1884. As if to say,] "Maybe, maybe not; at any rate it is a plausible thing and I may act as if she did."

298–300. "Is of a constant, loving, noble nature... A most dear husband."

[1884] Here his tone deepens into an almost honest tenderness befitting the words.

300. "Now, I do love her too..."

[1884] Rising and walking towards center front.

301–2. "... though peradventure/I stand accountant for as great a sin..."

Raising his eyes, and his right hand heavenward.

307–9. "And nothing can or shall content my soul ... yet that I put the Moor..."

Said with concentrated bitter emphasis.

311. "Which thing to do..."

---

10.   Booth cut 266–71 and 285–89.

Figure 11.   Photograph of Booth as Iago at the Drinking Song
(II.3.71–76)
Note the dagger dangling from a chain around his neck.
*(Courtesy of the Hampden-Booth Theatre Library at
The Players, New York City)*

[1884] Begins to speak with more rapidity.

Following 321. Exit Iago

[1884] Iago exits at right, up the steps and into the castle, the same way that Othello and Desdemona went [on their exit following 214].[11]

[Globe edition II.3]

26. "Well, happiness to their sheets!"[12]

53. "As my young mistress' dog. Now my sick fool Roderigo . . ."

Iago sits on seat in center.

64–65. "If consequence do but approve my dream, / My boat sails freely, both with wind and stream."

Turns and seems to speak this aside from those entering and to audience.[13]

71. "And let me the canakin clink, clink . . ."

While filling glasses.[14]

77. "I learned it in England, where, indeed, they are most potent in potting . . ."

Cassio drinks and Iago while talking to him in a gay manner, keeps filling up Cassio's glass; and Cassio drinks apparently without knowing how much.

Following 89. Iago empties his own glass on the ground.

---

11. Following the Herald's proclamation (see the note at the beginning of Act II above), Booth began II.3 of the Globe edition with Cassio greeting Iago (line 12). The dialogue between Othello and Cassio (1–8) had been transposed to II.1 following line 209. Booth cut Othello's greeting to Desdemona (8–11).

12. In the *Prompt Book* edition this reads "Well, happiness be theirs!" but Stone indicates that Booth said "Well, happiness to them both."

13. Following 64–65, the *Prompt Book* edition direction is "Re-enter Cassio; with him Montano and Gentleman."

14. Following Iago's line 70, "Some wine, ho!" the *Prompt Book* edition direction is "Enter Servant, with wine."

And walks off towards right front of the stage, coming back from which he sings second song [92–95], holding his glass.[15]

92. "King Stephen was a worthy peer..."

[1884] Booth lays more than usual stress on this song. Indeed, throughout this scene, he acts very well the part of a boon companion, while at the same time you see how carefully he is watching Cassio and leading him on in accordance with his own vile plans; Booth also shows Iago's amused contempt for the weakness of Cassio, his natural superficial amusement at Cassio or anyone's getting drunk and acting so silly, and his deeper satisfaction at seeing how perfectly his plans are working and how easily he can sway Cassio.

116. "Forgive us our sins!"[16]

Cassio kneels down.

117–18. "Do not think gentlemen, I am drunk..."

All exclaim, "O no!"

119. "I am not drunk now..."

All exclaim, "O no!" again.

122–123. "... you must not think then that I am drunk."

All exclaim, "O no!" again.

Following 123. Exit Cassio. All except Iago and Montano laugh and follow Cassio.

[1884] Left.

127–28. "He is a soldier fit to stand by Caesar/And give direction..."

---

15. Booth, following traditional practice, dropped the last verse, 96–99.

16. See Booth's note regarding Cassio's business (113–20) in the *Variorum*, 33.

[1884] Note the contrast of manner again. Now Booth assumes Iago's "good manner"—virtuous hypocrite!

157. "Away, I say; go out, and cry a mutiny."

Iago hustles poor Roderigo away very unceremoniously.

158–63. "Nay, good lieutenant... You will be shamed for ever."

[1884] Iago rushes about in excitement at right of stage and center, always in the background, while the gentlemen fight in front.

162. "The town will rise: God's will, lieutenant, hold!" [17]

[1884] With increased vehemence.

Following 163. Enter Othello and Attendants, from castle, and also the populace, at back. Gentlemen also re-enter L.

Enter Othello from doorway of Castle at right of stage. Cassio stands near doorway facing audience, seeming ashamed and half stunned. Montano wounded leans on stone seat in center, supported by two gentlemen. Iago walks back and forth at left of stage looking grieved and puzzled.

Othello's Dress: All white with long flowing sleeves; a sash of Turkish towelling embroidered with flowers and vine, ends aligned in front, sword with dark embossed wooden hilt. Hood lined with red, two large red tassels hanging below waist. Dark green velvet cap with jewel; turban of blue and white stripe. Shoes of purple, sparkling with jewels. Main point [is the] expression of regret, even sorrow at having to dismiss Cassio.[18]

[1884] Iago gets around to left corner front of stage by the pillar, and stands sword in hand(?), looking "dead with grieving" as Othello says [177].

179–87. "I do not know... to a part of it!"

---

17. Booth substituted "Heaven's" for "God's." He also cut 165 and 167–68. Othello's 164 and 166 were added to his speech 169–78.

18. This description taken from Stone's separate notes on Booth's performance as Othello.

Iago stands on left of stage. On finishing this speech he walks around stone seat among the populace and comes out on right of stage. Moonlight strikes his face.

[1884] Same as above as far as others go. But Iago stands still at left corner front, and does no walking about into moonlight, etc. But when answering Othello he steps a little towards him and stands facing Othello.

216. "In night, and on the court and guard of safety!"

Iago now stands on right of stage.

217. "'Tis monstrous. Iago, who began't?"

[1884] Iago still stands at left front corner, looking grieved and puzzled, as [above].

220. "Touch me not so near..."

Laying his hand on his sword.

[1881 and 1884] Third and fourth time I see Booth, he does <u>not</u> touch his sword, but simply waves his hand.

241. "But men are men; the best sometimes forget..."

In a tone as if appealing to Othello not to be hard on Cassio, and also looking from Cassio to Othello and back again.

248. "Cassio, I love thee..."

[1884] Iago makes a deprecating gesture of half dissent but with the utmost deference. Then he walks up stage a step or two and faces half to Othello, half to audience.

249. "But never more be officer of mine."

Iago shrugs his shoulders and an expression of triumphant delight flashes over his face, which he hides from lookers-on with his plumed hat in his hand.

255–56. "Iago, look with care... this vile brawl distracted."

[1884] Iago bows obedience, puts on his hat, and exits right, passing through the crowd of people standing around, with a proud mien.[19]

251. "Michael, I'll make thee an example."[20]

[1884] Cassio stands with his face dropped into his folded arms leaning on pillar at right near castle doorway.

259. "What, are you hurt, lieutenant?"

Hastening from left of stage over to Cassio.

[1884] Enter Iago who hastens over to Cassio and lays his hands on his shoulder with a tone and manner of sincere feeling, interest and sympathy.

266. "As I am an honest man . . ."

Seated on stone seat in center.

283. "O thou invisible spirit of wine . . ."

Clasping his hands, he [Cassio] rushes across stage in front of Iago to left of stage.

292–94. "O God that men should put an enemy in their mouths to steal away their brains!"

[Cassio] rushes back again.

296–97. "Why, but you are now well enough: how came you thus recovered?"

[1884] Nothing can exceed the naturalness of Booth's remarks and questions on this page, the blunt prosaic commonsense tones of Iago. Consider

---

19. Booth's note in the *Variorum* (145) is: "Iago goes off, Cassio braces himself for sentence, but sinks to the ground at Othello's exit [following line 256]. Iago hurriedly enters to Cassio" [at line 259]. Neither the *Prompt Book* edition nor any of Booth's working prompt books indicate this exit and entrance. The *Prompt Book* edition, for example, indicates "Exeunt all except Iago and Cassio."

20. Booth transposed this line, adding the "Michael," to follow 256. He also cut 251b, 252, and 257–58, the entrance of Desdemona.

how many thousand times he has asked these questions, and how can he repeat them so exactly as if for the first time? And as if he really wanted to know what he enquired?[21]

311–12. "Every inordinate cup is unblest, and the ingredient is a devil."

Rushes in same way again, to left of stage.

313–14. "Come, come, good wine is a good familiar creature if it be well used..."

Iago rises, goes to him, pats him on shoulder, etc.

[1884] Notice how courteous Iago is toward Cassio; I think Booth does not "pat him on shoulder"; there is none of that familiarity which has bred contempt, which is so conspicuous in his treatment of Roderigo.

314–15. "And, good lieutenant, I think you think I love you."

[1884] Cassio's back is toward Iago who looks toward him (they stand very near) with a searching expression and speaks in the tone of one who carefully weighs his words.

316. "I have well approved it, sir. I drunk!"

[1884] Cassio looks over his shoulder at Iago. [Then he] turns away again.

319. "Our general's wife is now the general..."

[1884] Cassio faces Iago and listens attentively.

323–24. "... confess yourself freely to her, importune her..."

[1884] Booth has a half smile in his voice.

---

21. Booth's note in the *Variorum* (146) on Iago's response to Cassio is: "Do not smile, or sneer, or glower—try to impress even the audience with your sincerity. 'Tis better, however, always to ignore the audience; if you can forget you are a 'shew' you will be natural. The more sincere your manner, the more devilish your deceit. I think the 'light comedian' should play the villain's part, not the 'heavy man,' I mean the Shakespearean villains. Iago should appear to be what all but the audience believe he is. Even when alone, there is little need to remove the mask entirely. Shakespeare spares you that trouble."

333–34. "I protest, in the sincerity of love and honest kindness."

Extending his hand to Cassio.

335. "I think it freely..."

They shake hands.

341. "Good night, honest Iago."

Shaking hands again warmly.

342–56. "And what's he then that says I play the villain? ... Directly to his good?"[22]

[1884] O, the exquisite sarcasm in his tone! And what a devilish smile! The whole makes one shiver!

356. "Divinity of hell!"

[1884] Then a sudden change to a serious tone in a burst like an oath.

368. "That shall enmesh them all."

[1884] Making an appropriate gesture with both hands clutching the air upwards with crooked up fingers spread.[23]

381. "And thou, by that small hurt, hast cashier'd Cassio."

Poking Roderigo in side; Roderigo looks delighted.

384–88. "By the mass, 'tis morning; ... Nay, get thee gone!"

[1884] Spoken very rapidly.

---

22. Booth cut, however, 345–54 from "For 'tis most easy ..." to "... With his weak function."
23. See III.3.241, note 19 below.

388. "Two things are to be done..."

[1884] Walking from right front corner to center.

Following 394. "Dull not device by coldness and delay."

Act III

Before the Castle, as in Act Second, Desdemona seated, and Cassio and Emelia discovered.

[Globe edition III.3. 480 lines cut to 439][1]

[1881] Third time that I see Booth, this scene is represented as a Moorish interior of the Castle, with rich curtains on rings hanging in front of arched doorways, with galleries running around, lounge, armchairs, etc. Desdemona is seated on the lounge.[2]

[1884] Fourth time same as third. Desdemona wears a lovely pale blue silk.

5. "O, that's an honest fellow. Do not doubt, Cassio . . ."

Turning to Emilia and taking her hand.

Following 34. Exit Cassio L. Enter Othello and Iago, at back.

Othello's Dress. Acts III and IV. Striped dress of black, scarlet, a steel color, and buff. Deep fringe on the flowing sleeves and on bottom of shirt; broad sash of a Roman silk scarf; dress more woolly. Undersleeves of white velvet elegantly embroidered with large raised work of flowers. Vest same as undersleeves; splendid rubies to button vest, through which white shirt shows a little and at wrists too. Necklace of magnificent jewels with a ruffle

---

1. Booth, following traditional practice, cut III.1 (58 lines) and III.2 (6 lines).

2. *Othello* #67 describes it as a "handsome interior." In some earlier and later productions, however, Act III was set in a "garden," or sometimes a room with a broad, raised, open gallery upstage center looking out into a garden or "cypress row" backdrop at the rear. But regardless of the setting, the blocking patterns and business remained essentially the same.

Figure 12.   Booth as Iago: "Ha! I like not that" (III.3.35)
Sculpture by John Rogers for which Booth posed, 1882.
(Courtesy of The New York Historical Society, New York City)

of white above it. Long purple stockings above knees; dress is looped up on left side with same jewels as above. Shoes as before, purple velvet sown with pearls apparently. Cap-turban as in Act I, purple velvet, with gold lace. The flaring sleeves are striped broader and not so many various colors, chiefly scarlet and gray. He has a dagger which he offers against Iago and then throws it away to center back.[3]

[1884] Cassio exits at center back right and delayed somewhat awkwardly so as to enable Othello and Iago to see it. [Then] enter at left corner front, Othello on Iago's right and a very little in advance, Othello perusing a large parchment document.[4]

35. "Ha! I like not that."

[1884] Said like an aside and yet very carefully so that Othello shall hear it.[5]

36. "Nothing my lord: or if—I know not what."

[1884] Like a person so truthful that even in such a trifle he would be scrupulously exact. From the instant of Booth's entrance in this scene every motion he makes, every syllable he utters, every note of his voice, deserves most careful study, for everything is intense with significance. And his facial expression not less so: to this no verbal description can give any idea; O, for a series of instantaneous photographs!

38. "Cassio, my lord?"

[1884] Booth starts and looks behind Othello's back off in the direction of Cassio's exit.

Following 40. Exeunt Iago and Emilia left.[6]

---

3. This description taken from Stone's separate notes on Booth's performance as Othello. See line 373, note 28 below, regarding use of this dagger.

4. Booth's note in the *Variorum* (161) is: "Desdemona and Emilia go with Cassio into the garden at back, and Cassio lingers just long enough to be seen by Othello and Iago. The women remain for a moment after his exit."

5. Booth's note in the *Variorum* (161) is: "Don't growl this,—let it barely be heard by the audience."

6. Booth's note in the *Variorum* (162) is: "Their presence would distract attention; besides, it is proper for them to retire during an interview between their superiors."

[1884] Exeunt center back toward right, just as Cassio did [at 34]. They walk off rapidly and close to each other.

91. "Excellent wretch! Perdition catch my soul..."[7]

Othello looking after Desdemona.

92. "Chaos is come again."

[Othello sits] center; reads paper.

[1884] Othello sits on end of lounge nearest footlights, with his back nearly towards Iago, and reads the paper he brought in with him.

93. "My noble lord,—"

On left of stage a little back of Othello. As he speaks, he approaches Othello and stands beside him. Throughout their scene, Iago speaks in a slow, calm, insinuating and apparently sincere tone and manner; and the consequent suspicion and convincement of Othello seem to follow naturally and inevitably from Iago's manner and words; you feel that Othello is justified in his opinion. Booth is very great here—and is as indescribable as he is inimitable. Iago handles in an absent manner the dagger which dangles from his necklace.

[1884] Iago has been standing respectfully apart in doorway of center back, while Othello and Desdemona finish their conference; [then] advancing toward Othello and halting near middle of stage.

104. "Honest! ay, honest."

Said as if it were preposterous to think otherwise; not emphatically at all.[8]

106. [Iago] "Think, my lord!"

---

7. Booth's note in the *Variorum* (166) is: "With joyousness—yet there should be an undertone of sadness,—as at their first embrace in Cyprus. Iago at the back of stage watches him with a sneering smile."

8. This description taken from Stone's separate notes on Booth's performance as Othello.

[1884] Spoken as if what he <u>thought might</u> be, and indeed [is], very different from what he <u>knew</u>, i.e., the opposite of Cassio's being honest.[9]

106. [Othello] "Think my lord!"

[1884] Othello walks off towards table and takes up something on it.

117. "My lord, you know I love you."

[1884] Said with such sweet sincerity and cordiality mingled with deference that it might deceive the very elect![10]

129. "Why, then, I think Cassio's an honest man."

[1884] In a tone implying "I wish I could believe him to be, but I can't." With what consummate art does Booth fit his manner to the words by which Iago by his very reluctance to speak excites the suspicions of the noble, open-hearted Moor! Then how admirable in his graceful deference towards Othello, made to spring from true friendliness of feeling as much as from the courtesy due to a superior officer. And his tones express sincere reluctance to wound Othello's heart by telling him his thoughts.[11]

146. "As, I confess, it is my nature's plague/To spy into abuses…"

[1884] He wriggles in the air with his finger, runs his neck outward and downward, stoops a little, and seems to be actually "spying into abuses."

155. "Good name in man and woman…"

[1884] Moving farther apart from Othello and delivering this speech in a noble manner according with the sentiments.[12]

---

9. Booth's note in the *Variorum* (168) is: "With embarrassment."

10. Booth's note in the *Variorum* (169) is: "Reproachfully."

11. Booth's note in the *Variorum* (171) is: "As though you would dismiss an unpleasant topic."

12. Booth's note in the *Variorum* (174) is: "Don't give this directly to Othello, but trust to the 'whiff and wind' of it, for your effect on him, and on the audience too, although it may not gain applause from them as do the scowls and growls of the stage villain."

161. "And makes me <u>poor indeed</u>."

"Poor" uttered with a prolonged emphasis and melody.

163. "You cannot, if my heart were in your hand..."

Making show as if it were.

164. "Nor shall not, whilst 'tis in my custody."[13]

Touching his own breast.

197. "Look to your wife; observe her well with Cassio..."

Approaches closer to Othello and seems to insinuate this in a lower tone.

206. "She did deceive her father, marrying you..."[14]

217. "Comes from my love; but I do see you're moved."

[1884] By tone and gesture of affection he expresses much loving sorrow here.

223. "Cassio's my worthy friend—"[15]

O what a lie!

225. "I do not think but Desdemona's honest."

Othello stands in front of lounge which stands across right end of stage, and he looks towards right, presumably towards the room where Desdemona is.

---

13. Booth's note in the *Variorum* (175) is: "Respectfully, not defiantly."

14. Stone refers back to her note at I.4.293: "Iago by a start and a malicious look shows that he takes heed of this remark, and you remember the future use he makes of it."—i.e., here at 206–8.

15. Booth's note in the *Variorum* (186) is: "Give this as a stiletto stab in the back—at which Othello groans aloud." In a note to Furness omitted from the *Variorum*, Booth wrote that he "violated the metre" on "My lord, I see you're moved" (224) by emphasizing the "you're"—"Othello having tacitly thrice denied the fact."

226. "Long live she so! and long live you to think so!"[16]

Fervently and <u>honestly</u> exclaimed!

[1884] Standing nearly in center door-way back, and lifting both hands heavenward.

227. "And yet, how nature erring from itself,—"[17]

[Othello] turning and walking towards center.

228. "Ay, there's the point: as—to be bold with you—"[18]

Stepping hastily forward and going close up to Othello and speaking with eagerness in Othello's ear.

241. "My lord, I take my leave."[19]

As he goes out, after turning away from Othello, he indulges in a diabolical look of fiendish exultation!

---

16. In a note to Furness omitted from the *Variorum* Booth wrote: "Perhaps a slight emphasis on *think*—I doubt its value."

17. Booth's note in the *Variorum* (187) is: "Referring to his color. (My father [Junius Brutus Booth] indicated this by a glance at his hand as it passed down before his eyes from his forehead where it had been pressed.) Iago seizes this with eagerness and interrupts him."

18. Booth's note in the *Variorum* (187) is: "My father interpreted this as a covert reference to Brabantio's assertion before the Senate (I.3.94) that Desdemona was 'a maiden never bold,' an assertion which Othello, with his knowledge of Desdemona's share in their wooing, might somewhat modify; my father, therefore, spoke the line not as it is usually printed, but as though catching up and pursuing Othello's own train of thought, and thus insidiously summoning to Othello's memory secret occasions when Desdemona had shown a 'will most rank,' and had been bold with him. I wish I could describe the white-lipped, icy smile, the piercing glance at Othello's half-averted face, and eager utterance, with which my father said, 'Ay, theres the point; as to be bold with *you.*'"

19. The *Prompt Book* edition indicates "Iago exits left." Booth's note in the *Variorum* (188) is: "A quick, fiendish smile of triumph and a rapid clutch of the fingers, as though squeezing his very heart (Othello's face is buried in his hands) is quite legitimate here, but do it unobtrusively, as you *vanish.*" Booth also employed this "clutching gesture" earlier at II.3.368.

[1884] The same. The previous acting has been <u>so fine</u> that spontaneous applause bursts from the audience loud and long continued, equal to a recall before the curtain, and interrupting the progress of the play.

Following 299. Re-enter Iago L.

[1884] Iago enters at left front corner and walks over to left side of the broad gallery doorway, rather indifferent towards Emilia. His tone sounds like the one usually employed by him towards his wife when they are alone. He leans upon the railing with one elbow, and looks out into the gallery.[20]

300. "How now? what do you here alone?"

In a surly tone, with his back partly turned to her, as he walks off toward left corner back of stage not perceiving the handkerchief.

301. "Do not chide; I have a thing for you."[21]

Emilia puts the handkerchief behind her.

306. "What handkerchief?"

Spoken carelessly and crossly.[22]

307. "What handkerchief!"

Emilia mocks his tone and manner.

308. "Why, that the Moor first gave to Desdemona . . ."

[1884] Iago leans on back of chair.

310. "Hast stol'n it from her?"

---

20. A similar pose is illustrated in figure 13.

21. Referring to "chide," Booth's note in the *Variorum* (162) is: "Note this. Iago's manner is brusque—disappointed at not finding Othello here; he had come to drive the dagger deeper in his heart."

22. Booth's note in the *Variorum* (195) is: "Indifferently. Upstage."

Figure 13.   Engraving of Booth as Iago, 1870
             *(Courtesy of the Hampden-Booth Theatre Library at
             The Players, New York City)*

Iago turns toward her, kneeling on the stone seat with one knee, leaning forward and expressing in his whole figure, face and gesture, eagerness to know if Emilia has got the handkerchief, and delight as he suspects she has and at last knows it.[23]

313. "A good wench; give it me."[24]

Iago approaches Emilia, puts his arm around her caressingly and kisses her.

315. "Why, what's that to you?"

In a quickly changed tone, a short, indifferent tone, and stepping hastily away from her to left of stage.

319. "Be not acknown on't; I have use for it."

Close to her again, shaking his finger in her face.

Following 320. Exit Emilia into Castle.[25]

Emilia pouts, shrugs shoulders, and makes a face at him as she goes out right.

321."I will in Cassio's lodgings lose this napkin..."

[1884] Sits down on chair at end of table, chair on whose back he leaned at [308]. Takes out of his pocket his own handkerchief, tucks Desdemona's in its place, and then puts his on top so it sticks out a little.

330. "Look, where he comes!"

---

23. Booth's note in the *Variorum* (195) is: "Turns quickly with delighted expectancy."

24. Booth's note in the *Variorum* (162) is: "Snatch at it eagerly." *Othello* #67 is marked "Attempts to get it." For line 315 in the *Variorum* (196) Booth's note is: "Pause mysteriously, 'Why'—as if about to give her some wonderful reason. Then snatch it, with 'What's that to you?'"

25. Booth's note in the *Variorum* (196) is: "Many Iagos kiss her, and coax her, to leave them—he is rather given to chiding than caressing."

Sitting down upon stone seat in center and watching Othello approaching, before the latter is seen by audience.

Following 333. Re-enter Othello.[26]

[1884] Iago takes up a book and opens it as if to make Othello suppose him quietly reading.

334. "Why, how now, general! no more of that."

Rising.

368. "If thou dost slander her and torture me..."

Othello rises, growing more and more angry, still clutching Iago.[27]

373. "Greater than that."[28]

Othello casts off Iago who staggers over to the left of the stage.

[1881] Third time I see Booth as Iago, in this scene, Othello knocks down Iago and stands over him a moment with uplifted arm; then rushes away to right back of stage.

---

26. Booth's note in the *Variorum* (198) indicates that Othello says "Ha! ha! false to me?" (333) "mournfully" while "Iago addresses him as though not expecting him" (334).

27. Following 360. "... give me the oracular proof," the *Prompt Book* edition indicates that Othello seizes Iago by the throat. In the preceding speech 348–57 "Farewell the tranquil mind, etc." Booth's note in the *Variorum* (200) is: "Begin slowly with suppressed emotion; gradually increase the volume and intensity of voice,—never loud, nor let you tones be too tearful or tremulous,—it becomes monotonous." And for the speech 359–68, Booth's note in the *Variorum* (203) is: "As before, with smothered intensity, not loud, gradually increasing, till 'If thou dost slander her'—when the full force of Othello's wrath breaks forth in violent tones and he seizes Iago who cowers."

28. Booth's notes in the *Variorum* (204) is: "I carry no weapon in this scene [i.e., as Othello], but seeing Iago's dagger I clutch it in frenzy and am about to stab him, when the Christian overcomes the Moor, and throwing the dagger from me, I fall again upon the seat with a flood of tears. To this weeping Iago may allude in his next speech, where he says contempously 'Are you a man?'" (374) Stone has indicated in her description of Iago's costume at the beginning of I.1 that a dagger in a case dangled from a large necklace that he wore. See figure 11. Stone indicated, however, in her note on his costume in 1883 that Othello did have a "dagger which he offers against Iago and then throws away to center back." See III.3.34 above.

[1884] This is not well done by the Othello so that the scene lacks fire and spirit.[29]

376. "... take mine office. O wretched fool..."

Approaching Othello and appearing to throw something down out of his hands before Othello.

381. "I'll love no friend, sith love breeds such offence."

Making a show of departing at left.[30]

392. "I see, sir, you are eaten up with passion..."

[1884] Some distance from Othello and on stage right.

394. "Would! nay I will."

[1884] Othello rushes up close to Iago.

413. "I lay with Cassio lately..."

Going close to Othello and speaking in a confidential manner.

421. "And then, sir, would he gripe and wring my hand..."[31]

Doing so to his own hand. Iago appears to mention the various circumstances which indicate Desdemona's guilt, with reluctance, and by no means as if he hated her, but because he is so devoted to Othello he cannot bear to have him abused. [See III.3.200. "Out of self-bounty be abused; look to't."] Also with somewhat of a lawyer's indifferent stating of evidence.

---

29. Othello was played by David H. Harkness (1836–1902). The critic of the *Boston Post* (21 February 1884) wrote that his "explosive tones" and "gutteral howls" would "do credit to an Egyptian dervish"; and in scenes "calling for excitement, he resembles ... an Indian chief enjoying ... a war dance."

30. Iago is stopped by Othello's "Nay, stay: thou shouldst be honest" (382). Booth's note in the *Variorum* (206), indicates that it should be said "Peremptorily, as to your subaltern, and Iago halts at the word of command."

31. *Variorum* (207): "Holds Othello's hand, which Othello draws with disgust from his grasp."

Othello in his excitement rushes about the stage a good deal, and Iago in speaking to him at different times turns in different directions according to Othello's position. Therefore Iago's part can't be written.[32]

433. "She may be honest yet. Tell me but this..."

Booth shows considerable eagerness.

Following 462. Iago kneels.

[Iago] kneels with wonderous grace, but instead of looking heavenward as he vows—as a good man would—he looks at Othello, rolling his eyes side-wise to do it as he faces audience.[33]

469. "I greet thy love..."

Puts his left arm around Iago and with his right clasps Iago's left hand.

Following 472–73. "... let me hear thee say/That Cassio's not alive..."[34]

Giving a start of surprise and horror.

[1884] Also.

---

32. *Othello* #67 indicates numerous crosses for both Othello and Iago beginning with line 427: "O monstrous! monstrous!" At "O monstrous!" Othello crossed from right center to left center. Iago countered from his left center position to center. At "I'll tear her all to pieces" (431) Othello crossed "up to center doors," but Iago stopped him and crossed to his left. Booth's note in the *Variorum* (208) is: "Here you may let the savage have vent,—but for a moment only; when Othello next speaks he is tame again and speaks sadly. Iago has caught and held him as he was about to rush off to 'tear her all to pieces.'" At "I gave her such a one" (436) Othello crossed to right center and Iago again countered by moving down left. This pattern of move and countermove continued then until each knelt at lines 460 and 462, respectively.

33. The *Prompt Book* edition indicates Othello kneels at "Swallow them up" [460]. Booth's note in the *Variorum* (208) is: "Kneels. Both hands above the head with upturned palms and fingers toward the back. I used this gesture impulsively, in England first, and it was spoken of as suggestive of the Orient. Iago watches Othello keenly—sidewise—during his next speech [462–69]; while Othello seems absorbed and with upturned eyes."

34. The *Prompt Book* edition indicates Iago "rises" with this line; Othello had already risen at 469. Booth's note in the *Variorum* (214) is: "Iago is shocked, of course, and slightly shudders as he rises to his feet."

474. "My friend is dead; 'tis done at your request . . ."

Then bows his head over Othello's hand and answers with an expression on his face of deep sadness and reluctance.

[1884] Turning again to Othello he wrings his hand and says these words in a voice choked with emotion.—The old hypocrite![35]

475. "But let her live."

[1884] After they have separated, and in a different tone.[36]

479. "For the fair devil. Now art thou my lieutenant."

Othello walks off right as if to go out.

480. "I am your own forever."

Rushing to Othello and kneeling to him with an expression of lively joy and utter devotion.[37]

---

35. *Othello* #67 is marked "Shakes hands with Othello."

36. Booth's note in the *Variorum* (214) is: "Beseechingly." The "separation" is undoubt-edly from the "embrace" and "handshake" indicated in the earlier lines (469 and 474).

37. Booth's note in the *Variorum* (214) is: "Iago shows deep grief, [476–79] till 'Now art thou my lieutenant.' Then, quickly kneeling, he kisses Othello's hand, and his face reveals his triumph." Booth's prompt book (*Othello* #59) indicates that the curtain was lowered on this "picture." Booth's note in the *Variorum* (214) is: "To portray Iago properly you must seem to be what all the characters think, and say, you are, not what the spectators know you to be; try to win even *them* by your sincerity. Don't *act* the villain, don't *look* it or *speak* it (by scowling and growling, I mean) but think it all the time. Be genial, sometimes jovial, always gentlemanly. Quick in motion as in thought; lithe and sinuous as a snake. A certain bluffness (which my temperament does not afford) should be added to perserve the military flavor of the character; in this particular I fail utterly, my Iago lacks the soldierly quality. My consolation is that we know him more as a courtier than as a soldier."

Act IV

Scene 1

The Same as in Acts Second and Third.[1]

[Globe edition III.4. 201 lines cut to 120]

108. "And lo the happiness! Go and importune her."[2]

Said with a sort of hateful glee!

132, 134, 139. "Is my lord angry?... Can he be angry? I have seen the canon... There's matter in't indeed, if he be angry."

This is all said in a most striking manner, in such an <u>honestly</u> surprised and anxious manner,—quite indescribable; it wins spontaneous applause from audience.

Following 139. Exit Iago L.[3]

---

1. Following traditional practice Booth cut Globe III.4.1–22. The *Prompt Book* edition locale refers to the "Scene in front of the castle" which Booth did sometimes use for both Acts II and III. At other times Act III was a "garden scene." In the productions Stone saw in 1881 and 1884, however, Booth's IV.1 was set undoubtedly in the "Moorish interior" of Act III described above. *Othello* #59, #65, and #67 all indicate "no wait" and "same scene as last Act." *Othello* #59, is marked "Garden Sc. cont. Move garden seat up to be closed in by Scene 2nd. See that table and chair in Sc. 2nd behind curtain or C. doors." *Othello* #67 also notes "See furniture above two"— i.e., above the position where they will be closed in by the second scene. In her note to Booth's IV.2.20 below, Stone indicates why the chair was to be set behind the curtain.

2. Stone's notes begin with Iago's entrance at line 107.

3. Booth transposed line 139 so that it immediately followed line 140, Desdemona's "I prithee, do so."

[1884] Crosses in front of Desdemona towards left to go out, —the same way that Othello went out [following 98].[4]

Scene 2

A Room in the Castle

[Globe edition IV.2.1–171. 171 lines cut to 152][5]

Center back—a crimson curtain.

20. "She says enough; yet she's a simple bawd."

Othello takes out a chair from behind the crimson curtain.[6]

42. "O Desdemona! away! away! away!"

Sits in chair.

96. "How do you, madam? how do you, my good lady?"

[Emilia] assists Desdemona to the chair in front of the crimson curtain.[7]

---

4. *Othello* #67 indicates that Othello exited through the right doorway.

5. Booth's IV.1 (Globe III.4) ended with Emilia's "Lady, amen" (165). Lines 166–69 were transposed to line 150. Booth followed traditional practice cutting various lines in Desdemona's speech 140–54, including 141–42, 145–48, and 150b–54. Booth, again following the usual practice, cut the remainder of Globe III.4 and IV.1. His IV.2 corresponded with Globe IV.2. See Hankey, *Plays in Performance: Othello,* op. cit., 263–79, for an excellent summation of how these scenes were variously cut and restored from 1755 onwards. *Othello* #67 is marked: "Scene second. A room in the Castle in 1st grooves. Center arch interior. Curtains on C. arch. Backed by interior. Tormentor doors on." *Othello* #59 describes it as "2. door Gothic in 2nd gooves." Sherwood also calls for a "Gothic" scene for an 1873 production at Booth's Theatre.

6. During Emilia's speech (12–19), Booth's note in the *Variorum* (255) is: "During this Othello is a little moved. He takes a chair from behind arras and sits." The actual sitting, however, seems to have occurred later. Both Stone and Booth (in a note omitted from the *Variorum*) indicate that Othello sat on line 42. Booth also indicates in a note omitted from the *Variorum* that Desdemona then knelt beside Othello. See, however, descriptions at lines 96, 115, 136, and 148–51 below. Booth changed "bawd" to "one."

7. Othello had exited following line 94.

Following 109. Re-enter Emilia with Iago L.1.E.[8]

[1884] Iago comes hurrying in (hat in hand) just as anyone would, if a friend, when so summoned; enters just before Emilia.

110. "What is your pleasure, madam? How is't with you?"[9]

Iago's manner towards Desdemona is full of sympathy and friendliness and deference, ever respectful tenderness and pity. Desdemona's touching appeals to him in words and by clasping his arm and taking his hands, combined with his manner and our knowledge of his <u>heart</u> and real deeds, make a pathetic and thrilling scene.

115. "Alas, Iago, my lord hath so bewhored her."[10]

[1881] Third time I saw Booth as Iago, he assists Desdemona to the chair.[11]

122. "Why did he so?"

To Emilia. Iago stands at Desdemona's left hand, a little behind her chair, on back of which he rests his right hand; his handsome profile shows against the crimson curtain to great advantage; his hat in hand.

130. "I will be hang'd, if some eternal villain..."[12]

Emilia does not look at Iago while she speaks, but stands at left of stage and a little in front of Iago. Iago rolls his eyes at her and casts on her a look of unutterable hate and anger, as if he'd like to choke her; yet slyly withal, and with a slight indication of an inward chuckle at her and Desdemona's ignorance of how sharply and aptly her words apply to himself; and overall in the veil of sarcastic indifference he always wears.

Following 133. "... I'll be hang'd else."

---

8.   "L.1.E." refers to "Left first entrance."

9.   In a note omitted from the *Variorum*, Booth calls for this line to be spoken "anxiously."

10.   Booth changed "bewhored" to "abused."

11.   She was then presumably helped only to her feet by Emilia at line 96 and then to the chair by Iago on this line.

12.   Booth's note in the *Variorum* (266) is: "This is spoken without intended reference to Iago."

[1884] Iago walks behind Desdemona's chair, so that at [134] he is standing on Desdemona's <u>right</u> side quite near her still. Booth makes Iago seem so sympathetic, so interested, so almost tenderly courteous towards Desdemona!

134. "Fie, there is no such man; it is impossible."

[As if to say,] "Fie, it's impossible, there is no such <u>fellow</u>."

135. "If any such there be, heaven pardon him!"

[Emilia] rising and moving towards right.

136–37. "A halter pardon him! . . . who keeps her company?"

During this speech, Iago puts the chair behind the crimson curtain and draws it close.[13] He also casts another of those sly looks of the essence of a devils's hate at Emilia.

143. "To lash the rascals naked through the world . . ."

[Emilia] crossing over as if to accompany Desdemona out.[14]

144. "Speak within door."

Approaching Emilia and speaking in a lower tone and crossly.[15]

145–47. "O, fie upon them! . . . with the Moor."

[1884] Standing on Iago's right hand.

144, 146, and 148. "Speak within door. . . . That turn'd your wit the seamy side without . . . You are a fool; go to."[16]

---

13. See note 17 for line 148, however. Booth cut 136b–37a.

14. *Othello* #67 and an omitted note from the *Variorum* indicate that Emilia crossed right on this line.

15. An omitted note from the *Variorum* indicates that Iago "goes to her and speaks low."

16. Booth's note in the *Variorum* (268) for "You are a fool," etc. is: "Angrily, but *sotto voce.*" *Othello* #67 indicates that Iago "X's to R & L behind Des." on line 148.

Are "asides" between Iago and Emilia.

148–51. "O, good Iago, ... here I kneel."

[1884] Still seated in chair, which, when she kneels [151], Booth puts behind curtain.[17]

154–58. "Or that mine eyes, mine ears, or any sense... To beggarly divorcement—love him dearly."

Iago spreads out his arms as if to save Desdemona from falling.

165. "I pray you, be content. 'Tis but his humor..."

[1884] Now on Desdemona's left side.

Following 171. Exeunt Desdemona and Emilia R. and Iago L.[18]

As Emilia goes out at right, Iago strikes at her angrily with his hat! Then crosses the stage with his own consummate grace of bearing, and goes out at left. The above by-play Booth omitted third time [1881] I saw him, and Iago made his exit at once at right. Emilia was a poor stick this time.[19]

Scene 3

Scene Third. A Dark Street. Iago's House.

[Globe edition IV.2.172–252 and V.1.1–129. 209 lines cut to 129]

---

17. *Othello* #67 indicates that Desdemona rose at line 148, then knelt. Iago then placed the chair behind the curtain. *Othello* #67 is further marked: "Clear chair and backing even as Iago places it behind." Obviously the exact line for initiating this sequence of Desdemona's sitting, rising, and kneeling, followed by Iago's removal of the chair changed over the years. *Othello* #67 also indicates that both Iago and Emilia helped Desdemona to rise at line 159, while Booth's note in the the *Variorum* (269) indicates that only Iago helped her to rise at line 165. See also Stone's note to lines 154–58.

18. Booth sometimes included here a portion of Desdemona's "Willow Song" scene (IV.3.23–57 and 106–7) here, but Stone indicates that it was omitted in performances she saw. *Variorum* (270): "Sometimes the scene ends here in which case, exit Iago with an angry glance at Emilia." Booth also cut Iago's 169–70.

19. Emilia was played by Mrs. Charles Calvert. See page 95, note 38.

[1881] Third time I see Booth as Iago, his house is in left corner back, and exits and entrances are changed to correspond. First time I see Booth as Othello (November 12, 1883) it is the same.[20]

[1884] House is left corner back.

Enter Iago from his house. Enter Roderigo, meeting Iago.[21]

Dressed as in I.1 without gloves. Roderigo is really quite angry. Iago cares not a whit for that.

198–202. "I tell you 'tis not very well . . . satisfaction of you."[22]

Roderigo begins this speech in a very brave and determined tone; Iago folds his arms and looks sternly in Roderigo's eye; the latter quails, and the last two or three words he utters in a changed tone of doubt, which is a comical contrast to that in which he begins.

[1881] Third time I see Booth as Iago, he does not fold arms, etc. as above.

206. "Why, now I see there's mettle in thee, and even . . ."

Iago slaps Roderigo on the shoulder.

209. "Give me thy hand, Roderigo . . ."

Iago tries to take Roderigo's hand; the latter is not disposed and turns away; but Iago persists, repeating the words and Roderigo yields.[23]

---

20. The *Prompt Book* edition and *Othello* #67 indicate that Iago's house was placed "R.U.E."—i.e., right upper entrance—but Sherwood indicates that in 1873 it was at "L. 3. E." Various sources call for "moonlight" for this scene.

21. Booth's note in the *Variorum* (270) is: "They run against each other,—Iago somewhat embarrassed. Roderigo refuses his proffered hand, and while the former is speaking 175. *et seq.*, Iago is somewhat nervous."

22. Booth's note in the *Variorum* (271) on "Well, go to; very well" (193) is: "With nonchalance, walking up and down, both here and at 197, but Roderigo's threat to make himself known to Desdemona arrests Iago, and he instantly plans the removal of Roderigo as well as Cassio." *Othello* #67 also indicates "up and down R." at these lines.

23. Booth's note in the *Variorum* (272) is: "Roderigo does not, but Iago wheedles, and gets his hand laughingly."

213. "I grant indeed it hath not appeared..."[24]

[1884] Booth says "it hath not <u>yet</u> appeared."

224. "Sir, there is especial commission come from Venice..."[25]

Iago takes Roderigo's arm with his left. Roderigo's anger has subsided and he seems ready again to listen to Iago's advice.

229–33. "O no; he goes into Mauritania ... the removing of Cassio."[26]

Extending his right hand and arm out from him in a slow peculiar manner, which Roderigo imitates [in] his tone and gesture.

236–37. "Why, by making him incapable of Othello's place..."[27]

Slapping his right hand down upon his left locked into Roderigo's arm.

[Globe edition V.1]

1. "Here, stand behind this bulk; straight will he come..."

[1884] Taking Cassio on one side towards right and back of stage.

4. "It makes us, or it mars us; think on that..."

Clapping Roderigo on the shoulder encouragingly.

---

24. Booth's note in the *Variorum* (272) calls for lines 213–21 to be said "Very earnestly."

25. Stone refers back to Desdemona's lines (IV.2.44–46), "If haply you my father do suspect/An instrument of this your calling back,/Lay not your blame on me . . ."

26. Booth's note in the *Variorum* (272) is: "Roderigo is elated at the thought of Desdemona's return to Venice, his home as well as hers; and is correspondingly disappointed when Iago says it is Mauritania. The 'removing of Cassio,' Iago speaks slowly, and mysteriously."

27. Booth cut 242–44 ("If you will . . . twelve and one") and 247–52 ("Come stand not . . . be satisfied") and all of IV.3, except the occasions when the "Willow Song" scene was transposed. He then transposed a reduced V.1 (Globe edition) to follow 247 (". . . between us") and simply continued the scene. These cuts and transpositions generally adhered to traditional nineteenth-century stage practice. Regarding IV.2.236–37 and 239–42, Booth's note in the *Variorum* (273) is: "Utter all this rapidly,—don't give Roderigo a chance to think."

Figure 14. Photograph of Booth as Iago (V.1.41–45)
*(Courtesy of the Hampden-Booth Theatre Library at
The Players, New York City)*

12–13. "Now, whether he kill Cassio, / Or Cassio him, or each do kill the other . . ."

Spoken in an undertone so that Roderigo does not hear.

19. "He hath a daily beauty in his life . . ."

Casting his eyes heavenward.

Following 22. Enter Cassio C.

[1884] Cassio must enter from the side opposite to Iago's house; in this case Cassio enters from right.[28]

Following 26. "O, I am slain!"

[Iago] rushes back into his house at right and shuts the door. Neither Roderigo nor Cassio knows it is Iago who thus stabs.

Following 41 and 45. "O, wretched villain! Nobody come? then I shall bleed to death."

Dress of Iago: white shirt, bare head, black and white checked cloak, flung around him, over one arm and covering most of his legs, a lighted candle in one hand and his sword in the other.

Following 61. "O murderous slave! O villain!"

---

28. The action of wounding Cassio and Roderigo is fairly complicated. Following is a summary description drawn from the stage directions in the *Prompt Book*, *Othello* #67, and Booth's notes in the *Variorum*. At ". . . be bold, and take thy stand" (7), Iago retires a "little distance" and then exits "into his house," while Roderigo takes his "stand" upstage, but presumably opposite Iago's house. For his speech (12–22) Iago appears in his doorway. With Cassio's entrance, Roderigo rushes from his post and makes a pass at Cassio. They then fight and Cassio wounds Roderigo. At "O, I am slain!" (26) Iago comes from his doorway and first strikes away Roderigo's sword and then cuts Cassio behind the leg and rushes out. (Booth then cut 28–36, 38–40, 42–44, 46–52.) Following "O wretched villain! Nobody come? then I shall bleed to death" (Booth cut 43–44), Iago re-enters, dressed as Stone describes him, and with a light (see fig. 14). At "O murderous slave!" (61) Iago stabs Roderigo. "Cassio takes Desdemona's handkerchief from his pocket and binds his leg." Roderigo faints and at "How silent is this town!" (64), he is "about to stab Cassio" when he "sees Lodovico and Gratiano approaching." To enhance the mood of this scene, Booth gradually worked the "moonlight" off beginning with Cassio's entrance. Hence the need for Iago's lamp. Lodovico and Gratiano were accompanied by torchbearers and with their entrance, moonlight was gradually worked back on.

Iago turns his sword around in Roderigo's breast with a fiendish look!

64. "How silent is this town! Ho! murder! murder!

At this point—or just after it—the sudden gleam of the devilish thought is seen on Iago's face that now is a chance for him to murder Cassio too and escape suspicion; and with his sword drawn, he darts towards Cassio; but Lodovico and Gratiano appear too quickly.

72 and 88. "Marry, Heaven forbid! / Know we this face or no?"[29]

[1884] With lamp in hand he stoops over Roderigo.

90. "Roderigo? no:—yes, sure;—O, heaven! Roderigo."

[1884] Kneels down and bows his face upon the hilt of his sword as if overwhelmed with sorrow!

112. "Cassio hath here been set on in the dark . . ."[30]

[1884] Lifting his head and speaking with a voice of mingled grief, astonishment, and anger. I think he does not rise.

126. "Emilia, run you to the citadel."

[1884] Iago is standing now with back to the audience.

128. "Will you go on? I pray." [Exeunt all but Iago]

[1884] In a tone which betrays to <u>audience</u> his great desire to get rid of them.[31]

128–29. "This is the night / That either makes me or fordoes me quite."

Iago stands in center of stage, stooping forward with an eager look, one-third apprehensive, two-thirds exultant, flourishing his sword. He speaks with intense force, and makes a striking tableau.

---

29. Following traditional practice Booth cut 73–87, Bianca's entrance.

30. Booth cut 91–110, so Emilia entered following 90. He also cut 116–25.

31. Booth's note in the *Variorum* (291) is: "Watch them well off, then take a look at Roderigo and speak hoarsely."

Act V

A Bedchamber in the Castle, Raised Bed L, opposite to large Window R. Moonlight streams through Window and falls upon Bed. Door C. Ottoman C. A Light burning on Table. Desdemona in Bed, asleep, discovered. Othello also discovered.[1]

[Globe edition V.2. 371 lines cut to 300]

Othello's dress. White gown with long flowing sleeves and white linen undersleeves; hood lined with red and [with red] tassels. But his sash is different, and I notice up and down the front a curious crimson lacing. At opening of scene, he has a cloak partially around him, one end trailing, black and grey striped. No turban or cap. A dagger concealed in his bosom.

Othello discovered at window right, raising left hand starward, on which moonlight and firelight mingled shines.[2]

2. "Let me not name it to you, you chaste stars!"

Draws the curtains, making the room perceptibly darker. Glances towards her. The table is [on the left] between door at center back and front of bed, and on it is a candle.

---

1. Booth's note in the *Variorum* (292) is: "I prefer the bed at the side of the stage with the head towards audience, because it is of more importance that Othello's face should be seen than Desdemona's dead body, and the killing is partly hidden by the arrangement." For a brief history of how this scene was staged in the nineteenth century, see Hankey, 307–8, and James R. Siemon, "'Nay, that's not next': *Othello*, V.2. in Performance, 1760–1900," *Shakespeare Quarterly* 37 (Spring 1986): 38–51. This description coincides with the groundplan in *Othello* #67.

2. I have incorporated into this act Stone's notes on both Othello and Iago.

3. It is the cause. Yet I'll not shed her blood . . . "

Half drawing and then relinquishing his dagger. He seems settled in his mind to kill her, but undecided as to <u>how</u>. He strides towards her and then stops.

4–5. "Nor scar . . . monumental alabaster."

Standing behind table in center wrapping his cloak over one arm. (There is another table at center.)

6. "Yet she must die, else she'll betray more men."

Walking towards side-table [left] and sitting down in front of it with back towards audience.

7. "Put out the light, and then put out the light."

Making motion with right hand as if to extinguish the lamp.

10. " . . . but once put out thy light . . ."

Looking towards bed and gesticulating towards her, stretching his arms towards her. Tone of sad resignation.

13. "When I have plucked the rose . . ."

Rising and approaching the bed by ascending the two steps of the dais on which it is placed.

16–17. "Ah, balmy breath . . . One more, one more."

Kissing her, each time more passionately. Voice and manner are expressive of a world of tenderness and love towards Desdemona.

20–21. "I must weep, / But they are cruel tears . . ."

Gathering up his tears with his peculiar gesture of his hands at his eyes.

22. "She wakes."

Hastily descending the steps, and striding towards other side of the room.

23 and 25. "Ay Desdemona / Have you pray'd tonight, Desdemona?"[3]

Spoken in a harsh, cold, authoritative tone and manner.

26–28. "If you bethink ... Solicit for it straight."

In a changed and lower tone as if to himself and with heartfelt earnestness.

32. "... heaven forfend!"

Lifting both hands heavenward and looking up.

62–66. By heaven ... I saw the handkerchief."[4]

Not in a tone of ordinary petulant anger, but in a tone of deep settled righteous indignation and determination.

71–72. "No, his mouth ... ta'en order for't."

Said as he walks on left of center table <u>upstage</u> away from audience. Walks around table and comes down stage again, exclaiming the next speech [74–75] in very passionate manner with arm extended and hand clutching upwards into the air, and an expression of fierce hate against Cassio.

77–83. "Out, strumpet ... It is too late."

Rushing to the bedside. I think after Desdemona is "smothered" that Booth remains crouching by the bed with his head buried in the curtains until the knocking is heard. As he stabs her there is an expression of agonized loathing at his own deed and its necessity so vividly portrayed in his face, as he hangs his head and does not look at his own dagger nor at her, that it seems as if he could hardly do it.[5]

---

3. Booth omitted Desdemona's "Will you come to bed, my lord?" (24).

4. Booth cut lines 68–70.

5. Booth changed "strumpet" to "wanton." At line 52, according to Booth's note in the *Variorum* (299), "Desdemona comes from her bed and rests trembling against it." Desdemona sinks to her knees at line 57 and then down to line 77 "she is half reclining on the steps and dais of the bed." Following line 79 an "enraged" Othello struggles

Following 166. Emilia rushes out center, and re-enters, followed by Montano, Gratiano, and Iago, C., with attendants.

[1884] Iago enters last. Wears a new suit which has a striking appearance. Legs are same, but he has on a tunic of black velvet, cut very open at the neck and down the breast to show white shirt. Sleeves of gray velvet and on upper part shirred bands or puffings of rose-colored silk. Sword belt of reddish gold color and quite like a sash. He is paler than ever before, and his cheeks are daubed with darkish color to make them look hollow. Hat same as before, carried in his hand.

169–70. "O, are you come, Iago? . . . murders on your neck."[6]

Iago stands at right front part of stage, while the others are grouped on left, behind and around Othello. As he takes his position, the footlights are brightened so as to show him distinctly; hat in hand.

174. "I know thou didst not, thou'rt not such a villain . . ."

[1884] Poor Emilia! Iago <u>was</u> fascinating when he chose to be.

175. "Speak, for my heart is full."[7]

She lays her head on his shoulder.

176. "I told him what I thought, and told no more . . ."

---

with Desdemona, hiding her "from the audience while she gets back upon the bed" (*Variorum* 301). The *Prompt Book* edition indicates that Booth smothered Desdemona at 83, then there was a "long pause." Emilia is then heard knocking "not . . . loud" (*Variorum* 302) at the center door. Adhering to a practice begun in the eighteenth century and continued throughout the nineteenth century, Booth stabbed Desdemona at 87, "So, so." Booth's note in the *Variorum* (303) is: "Hide your face in trembling hand while you stab and groan 'So, so'; the steel is piercing your own heart." For a survey of this stage business in the nineteenth century theatre, see Sprague, *Shakespeare and the Actors,* 212–16, and Hankey, 316–19. Stone wrote no comments between 83 and 166.

6. Booth's note in the *Variorum* (314) is: "Iago, of course, is much astonished." At 170, "Othello goes to bed and lies moaning there, not loudly."

7. Booth's note in the *Variorum* (314) is: "Iago hardens himself, as it were, looking straight before him; immovable,—and answers after a pause, and doggedly."

[1884] He shows from the first a sullen fierce effrontery, a determination to have it out, veiled under a cold soberness of mien as like as possible to what he might wear if Desdemona had been guilty. Thus at 176, 179 and 183.[8]

194. "What, are you mad? I charge you, get you home."

[1884] This is virtually an "aside" to Emilia, though not so designated. At ["I charge you..."] his anger blazes up, anger mixed with astonishment at Emilia's rebelling against him at this late hour.

197. "Perchance, Iago, I will ne'er go home."

[Emilia] sitting down on seat in center and dropping her head, and sobbing.[9]

[1884] Addressed to Iago, but without regard to its being overheard by others. Strange presentiment! The use of "will" instead of "shall" would indicate her thought to be that she would not live as wife with such a villian any longer; "perchance"—i.e., perhaps she should not be able to bring her mind to endure him.

218. "O heaven! O heavenly powers!"

[Emilia] rising and throwing up her arms wildly.[10]

225–26. "... that handkerchief thou speakest of/I found by fortune and did give my husband..."

Iago starts, begins to tremble—first perceived in the shaking of the plumes in the hat he holds in his right hand over his left arm. Increases violently. He seems to turn pale and looks frightened, opens his mouth once or twice, as if gasping, and fumbles at the fastening of his doublet at the throat.[11]

---

8. At 179, Booth's note in the *Variorum* (314) is: "Short and sharp. He darts a quick glance at her in defiance, but quails as she proceeds, and speaks 183 ['With Cassio, mistress'] with desperation." Booth cut 183–93, "Go to, charm your tongue ... O villainy, villainy!"

9. Booth's note in the *Variorum* (316) is: "Iago gloats over this quietly. Emilia sits on divan, center."

10. Booth cut 219–25: "Come, hold your peace ... O thou dull Moor!"

11. Following 235 the *Prompt Book* edition indicates: "Iago stabs Emilia. Othello assaults Iago and is disarmed by Montano. Iago runs out C. Emilia is supported by an attendant, who assists her to a couch in front of window."

243. "I am not valiant neither..."

Standing just at right of center back.

249. "Moor she was chaste..."

[Othello] striding across stage behind table to Emilia to hear what she has to say.

249. "... she loved thee, cruel Moor..."

[Othello] bending over Emilia and hidden by curtains almost entirely. Then he turns around [and] clutches curtain nearest footlights with his left hand.

Following 251. "So speaking as I think, I die, I die."

[Othello] walking towards footlights.

252. "I have another weapon in the chamber..."

[Walking] around table to right corner.

253. "It is a sword of Spain, the ice-brook's temper..."

Standing at door center back.

254. "O, here it is."

Winding his sleeves up around his right arm so its drapery shall not interfere with wielding it.[12]

254. "Uncle, I must come forth."

Flourishing sword <u>slightly</u> and holding it erect before himself.

259. "Behold I have a weapon..."

Pointing sword towards Gratiano, straight and so determinedly as to convey impression of darting it towards him. Slightly shaking "this little arm" [262] and touching it with his left hand.

---

12. The *Prompt Book* edition indicates "Takes a sword from recess near bed."

261. "Upon a soldier's thigh..."

Slapping his left thigh with left hand.

271. "Where should Othello go?"

Dropping his sword point downward on floor and leaning on it.[13]

273. "... when we shall meet at compt..."

[He] is half kneeling on steps and looking heavenward.

275. "Cold, cold, my girl!"

Feeling her hand and arm.

277. "Whip me, ye devils..."

Rising and frantically clasping his head and gesticulating.

281–82. "O Desdemona! Desdemona! dead!/O! O! O!"

Throwing himself with despairing abandon again upon his knees beside the bed, his whole figure expressive of his striken grief; same position as he assumed at [170] only he somehow expresses a subtle difference now, a more restless and intense agony, the mingling of remorse with sorrow at her death. The agony of his cry is heart-rending and his gestures express even more so.[14]

Following 285. Iago is brought in.[15]

Iago's hands are tied behind him, he twists and struggles and succeeds in partially freeing his right arm. He stands right-front, near center seat. Looks

---

13. Booth's note in the *Variorum* (322) is: "Goes towards bed, near which his sword falls from his hand."

14. In a note omitted from the *Variorum*, Booth wrote: "Sink utterly prostrated by his agony. After a pause, the characters [i.e., Ludovico, Montano, Cassio, and officers] enter slowly; Cassio, supported, has the handkerchief around his leg."

15. Booth's note in the *Variorum* (323) is: "Othello draws the bed curtains close at Iago's entrance, that Desdemona's corpse may not be polluted by Iago's gaze. All eyes are fastened on Iago thus giving Othello the chance to assault him unobserved."

Figure 15.   Photograph of Booth as Iago (V.2.285)
            (Courtesy of the Hampden-Booth Theatre Library at
            The Players, New York City)

like the baffled fiend he is, sullen that he has been discovered in his treachery and hence prevented from reaping all the profits, yet fiercely exultant in the evil he has wrought for others, and proud after all, in his own intellectual superiority.

287. "If that thou be'st a devil, I cannot kill thee." [Wounds Iago.]

Rushing from dais towards Iago with a look of vengeance and distress fearful to behold.

288. "I bleed, sir, but not kill'd."

Exultant that Othello has not succeeded in full revenge, Iago bends over, stuffs his handkerchief in a wad into his side where he is wounded, actually grows pale, looks faint, staggers a little, but still bears his indomitable air and atmosphere of hate.

289. "I am not sorry neither: I'd have thee live..."

With head slightly bent towards Iago, and eyes looking up at him in the peculiar Othello style of Booth.

290. "For, in my sense, 'tis happiness to die."[16]

Said very quietly. From speech [243] onwards, Othello wears air of being stunned, stupefied, bewildered by the circumstances, a slight air pervading all he does and says.

293–94. "Why, anything:/An honorable murderer if you will..."

Said facing audience more, but not looking at them. Lifting both hands upward and spreading them aloft, and looking heavenward, lifting his head up too, with an expression and voice of keenest agony. Othello flings himself down in chair by table towards left and his head falls on his breast. Somewhow the impression is conveyed to me that Othello thinks not only that "it is happiness to die" because he cannot bear the agony of life now,

---

16. Booth's note in the *Variorum* (323) is: "''Twere now to die, 'twere now to be most happy.' The same sad refrain first heard in the very heaven of her happiness, now in his hell of misery. Let it be faintly heard whenever possible through your performance of this character."

and because he deserves death, but also that he can so, and only so, again commune with Desdemona and tell her his remorse and how it was he did kill her. His deliberation and tones are fine here.

Notice whenever (or usually) when Booth "sheds tears" he so covers his eyes that no one can see that no real tears fall; and also that on removing his hand and resuming speech, he gulps and speaks the first word or second with difficulty, as a person would naturally.

295. "For naught I did in hate, but all in honor."

Spoken with great distinctness and unction.

303. "Demand me nothing: what you know, you know..."

These words are thrown at them all between his teeth, especially at Othello.[17]

304. "From this time forth I never will speak word."

Most of the time Iago's head is hanging down in sullen brooding and reckless despair of the wicked who are found out in their wickedness and all their schemes come to naught. The wound given him by Othello has evidently hurt him considerably, he staggers and grows paler, but will not yield, keeps trying to straighten up and defy everybody, determined not to afford his enemies the satisfaction of seeing him overcome. The drooping of his head is partly caused by physical weakness. It is quite noticeable how utterly he is neglected by all, everybody shuns him, avoids approaching him as if he were a leper.

The look of determination that settles on his face contains various emotions and is <u>indescribable.</u>

[1884] Same as usual, only if possible it is given with more of that slow, stern, inflexible bitterness, of ugliness that still opposes good, if no longer by active fighting, since that is no longer possible, then by its own weight hanging sullenly upon the skirts of justice.

Following 337. An officer removes Iago from where he stands, to the body of his wife at the window.

---

17. Booth's note in the *Variorum* (324) is: "I grind my teeth at this, not because it 'takes' but because I feel it expresses determination never to speak again."

Iago's back is to audience and the attendant stands between audience and him also, so we cannot see how he is affected—if at all.

[1881] Third time I see Booth as Iago, he is removed by officer to ottoman at center of stage, and half reclines on it with back to audience. When Othello stabs himself, [356] he falls in front of ottoman, and Iago twists himself around and glares upon Othello with a look of fiendish triumph.[18]

[1884] Iago is presumably guarded by an officer who stands near, but without touching him. I think his backward movement and dropping onto a circular couch near middle of stage is a voluntary one caused by physical hurt; he drops his head, and his whole attitude indicates bodily abandonment by its awkward stiffness. His face is hidden, but his labored breath is seen in arm and legs.

Following 356. Iago starts forward in wicked triumph. He is seized by an officer who forces him to his knee.[19]

[1884] Taking him by the throat with one hand, and choking him till the blood flushes into his face.

---

18. In a note omitted from the *Variorum,* Booth writes: "Iago glares with a triumphant smile at Othello, who slowly recoils from his gaze and sinks with his face buried in the curtains of the bed." Booth's note in the *Variorum* (332) is: "At the word 'thus' [356: 'And smote him, thus'] Othello stabs himself, cries 'O, Desdemona,' makes an effort to reach the bed, clutching (not much) for the curtains as he falls back dead."

19. Booth ended the play with line 357: "O bloody period! / All that's spoke is marr'd."

Appendix

Figure 16. Booth as King Lear: "You are a spirit, I know: When did
you die?" (IV.7.49)
Sculpture by John Rogers for which Booth posed, 1885.
(Courtesy of The New York Historical Society, New York City)

Booth's King Lear

At the end of Act I and at the close of the performance, my first and perhaps my strongest impression is one of disappointment, at least that feeling is uppermost. Much of this is owing to my intense enjoyment of Mr. Booth's own personality and the more this is concealed by the exigencies of the character he assumes, by just so much is my enjoyment lessened. Then the support is so miserably poor and inadequate (with the exception of Edgar and the Fool) that the play as a whole on the stage seems far inferior to the same when read. There is no sort of harmony, no en rapport, between Booth and the other actors beyond the merest surface polish; they are in short utter "sticks."[1] The part of Lear does not seem so thoroughly the play of itself as does Hamlet. All through the performance I am haunted by a strange resemblance to some familiar face. Could it be that of W.P.T.[2] as being the only man known to me wearing the white beard and mass of white hair that Booth does on this occasion?

What special parts stand in my memory as revealed most vividly? Or what were the most touching? Which the electrical passages? Not the famous "Curse of Goneril" scene. He spoke too rapidly and too weakly. If anything it is after the advent of Poor Mad Tom where Lear's wits begin to unsettle, and insanity is plainly developed. You can see Lear's expression

---

1. During Booth's two weeks at the Globe Theatre, 5–27 November 1883, the Boston critics were unusually severe about his poor support. When Booth moved on to New York on 10 December, the New York critics continued this attack on Booth's support. Edgar was played by Eben Plympton (1853–1915), and the Fool by Owen Fawcett (1839–1904). Both of these actors had long stage careers playing supporting roles not only for Booth, but for Lawrence Barrett, Modjeska, John McCullough, and other "stars."

2. I have been unable to identify "W.P.T." He was probably a family friend or acquaintance.

change from that of a man sore-stricken with getting excited to that of an actually crazy old man. I am impressed with the idea that the final over-throw of the wavering balance is caused by the witnessing of Tom's crazy appearance and talk which evidently make a profound impression upon Lear. This was not at all suggested by reading the play, but only by Booth's acting. (The difficulty of hearing distinctly even Booth's fine articulation makes me think how delightful it would be to hear him act in a small hall, where he need not so strain his voice, and where all the exquisite delicate modulations could be fully appreciated!)

III.4.153–58. "Go in with me ... fire and food is ready."

Lear sits, pulls one or two pieces of straw out of Poor Tom's straw crown and plays with it, examines it minutely, and shows his mind is fast unset-tling. During Gloster's address to Lear, Lear appears to be too interested in Edgar and he strains to understand what is said to him; he evinces none of his previous emotion when his daughters are mentioned; and yet he appears to listen, but yet is too crazy to understand.

IV.7.37–38. "Mine enemy's dog ... fire ..."

She addresses to Kent turning around away from the couch.

44. "How does my royal lord? How fares your majesty."

Cordelia speaks her lines very slowly and loudly so that it seems ridiculous that Lear does not far sooner awaken with so much declamation going on at his ear!

46–49. "You do me wrong ... when did you die?"

Are spoken lying down and very faintly.

52. "Where have I been? Where am I? Fair daylight?"

He sits up on the couch.

55. "I will not swear these are my hands..."

He looks at and feels of his hands.

59–63. "Pray do not mock me ... my perfect mind."

This said in a most touching tone and manner. He picks up the tassel of his robe and plays with it, picking it apart, and looking at it aimlessly.

64. "Methinks I should know you, and know this man."

Looking at Cordelia who stands right and then at Physician.

67. "Remembers not these garments…"

Taking hold of his robe with both hands and slightly raising it. It is a dun, plum colored robe, lightish with collar and cuffs of dark fur or plush, and tied around the waist with cord and tassel; buttoned in front with conspicuous metallic buttons.

69–70. "For, as I am a man… child Cordelia."

Again the "recognition scene" is very fine; the transition from weak, wavering re-awakening of his faculties to the—as it were—sudden leap of Reason to her throne again, and his emotion of intense joy at recognizing her, all is wonderfully expressed! How his eyes actually dilate and darken and blaze and with what a wondrous smile and piercing sweetness of tone he exclaims "I think this lady to be my child!"

Selected Bibliography

Bratton, J. S., ed. *King Lear: Plays in Performance*. Bristol: Bristol Classical Press, 1987.

Carlson, Marvin. *The Italian Shakespearians*. Washington, D.C.: Folger Shakespeare Library, 1985.

Cohen, Richard. "Hamlet as Edwin Booth." *Theatre Survey* 10 (May 1969): 53–74.

Furness, Horace Howard, ed. *A New Variorum Edition of* Hamlet. Philadelphia and London: J. B. Lippincott Company, 1877.

_____. *A New Variorum Edition of* Othello. Philadelphia and London: J. B. Lippincott Company, 1886.

Grossman, Edwina Booth. *Edwin Booth: Recollections by His Daughter and Letters to Her and to His Friends*. New York: The Century Company, 1894.

Hankey, Julie, ed. *Othello: Plays in Performance*. Bristol: Bristol Classical Press, 1987.

Lockridge, Richard. *Darling of Misfortune: Edwin Booth, 1833–1893*. New York and London: The Century Company, 1932.

Mills, John A. *Hamlet on Stage: The Great Tradition*. Westport, Conn.: Greenwood Press, 1985.

_____. "The Modesty of Nature: Charles Fechter's Hamlet." *Theatre Survey* 15 (May 1974): 59–78.

Rosenberg, Marvin. *The Masks of King Lear*. Berkeley: University of California Press, 1972.

_____. *The Masks of Othello*. Berkeley: University of California Press, 1961.

Ruggles, Eleanor. *Prince of Players: Edwin Booth*. New York: W. W. Norton & Company, Inc., 1953.

Shattuck, Charles H. *The Hamlet of Edwin Booth*. Urbana: The University of Illinois Press, 1969.

_____. "The Romantic Acting of Junius Brutus Booth." *Nineteenth-Century Theatre Research* 5 (Spring 1977): 1–26.

_____. *Shakespeare on the American Stage: From the Hallams to Edwin Booth*. Volume 1. Washington, D. C.: Folger Shakespeare Library, 1976.

_____. *Shakespeare on the American Stage: From Booth and Barrett to Sothern and Marlowe*. Volume 2. Washington, D.C.: Folger Shakespeare Library, 1987.

_____. *The Shakespeare Promptbooks: A Descriptive Catalog*. London and Urbana: The University of Illinois Press, 1965.

Siemon, James R. "'Nay, that's not next': Othello, V.2 in Performance, 1760–1900." *Shakespeare Quarterly* 37 (Spring 1986): 38–51.

Sprague, Arthur Colby. *Shakespeare and the Actor*. Cambridge, Mass.: Harvard University Press, 1944.

_____ . *Shakespearian Players and Performances*. Cambridge, Mass.: Harvard University Press, 1953.

Watermeier, Daniel J. "Edwin Booth's Iago." *Theatre History Studies* 6 (1986): 32–35.

_____ . "Edwin Booth's Richelieu." *Theatre History Studies* 1 (1981): 1–19.

_____ , ed. *Between Actor and Critic: Selected Letters of Edwin Booth and William Winter*. Princeton: Princeton University Press, 1971.

Watermeier, Daniel J. and Ron Engle. "Booth and Dawison's Polyglot *Othello*." *Theatre Research International* 13 (Spring 1988): 48–56.